Buddha Heart, Buddha Mind

BUDDHA HEART, BUDDHA MIND

■ ■ ■ ■

LIVING THE FOUR NOBLE TRUTHS

HIS HOLINESS
The Dalai Lama

TRANSLATED FROM THE FRENCH BY
ROBERT R. BARR

A Crossroad 8th Avenue Book
The Crossroad Publishing Company
New York

The Crossroad Publishing Company
481 Eighth Avenue, New York, NY 10001

Originally published under the title Pacifier L'Esprit
©1999 by Editions Albin Michel, S.A., Paris

English translation copyright © 2000 by
The Crossroad Publishing Company

Printed in the United States of America

Library of Congress Cataloging-in-Publication Data
Bstan-®dzin-rgya-mtsho, Dalai Lama XIV, 1935-
Buddha heart, Buddha mind : living the Four Noble Truths.
p. cm.
Includes bibliographical references.
ISBN 0-8245-1866-7 (alk. paper)
1. Buddhism—Doctrines. 2. Religious life--Buddhism. 3. Dge-lugs-pa
(Sect)—Doctrines.   I. Title.
BQ7935.B774 B8 2000
294.3'444—dc21
00-011096

1 2 3 4 5 6 7 8 9 10 04 03 02 01 00

Book design by Stefan Killen Design

Contents

■ ■ ■ ■

Expressions of
Gratitude and Homage
■ ■ ■ ■

HOMAGE TO MANJUSHRI OF JOUVENCE!

This book contains eight addresses given by His Holiness, the Fourteenth Dalai Lama, from April 26 through 29, 1997, at the Institut Karma Ling, near Arvillard, in Savoie, France.

Jigmé Khyentsé Rinpoché not only transcribed the addresses and the questions and answers but also has tirelessly polished the translator's lantern: for this, warm thanks, as well as, for their lights, to Kusho Lhagdor and Matthieu Ricard.

Homage to this Ocean Repository of Teachings, Avalokita himself, by whom extraordinary agility of body and mind dissolve resistance to the good! May the magic of his utterance pacify our anguish. May he live as long as the mountains and rivers!

Introduction:
Laying the Groundwork
■ ■ ■ ■

I should like to say to all of you how glad I am of this opportunity to meet with you to exchange some words and views. I am very happy that you are interested enough to come in such great numbers. Those who have prepared for this event have truly done so in a grand way, and I thank them for it. During these preparations, difficulties have never been wanting. But you have never shirked the task, and I am very happy for this.

Beginning today, we shall meet eight times to speak of the Dharma. I shall present Buddhism to you essentially on the basis of the Four Noble Truths. I shall proceed as if we already had a spiritual connection, as I have always done when I have given an address on Buddhism. At the conference's conclusion we shall all take the vow of the spirit of Awakening. That is the priority of Buddhists, and what will naturally create a spiritual connection among us.

THE NEED TO REFORM OUR MIND

Why are we gathered here today? Not for business, and not to

attend a spectacle or show. The essential thing for today is to listen
to a Buddhist address. To what end? To reform our mind. What
must be reformed in our mind?

Generally speaking, among all animals that experience themselves as an "I," the avoidance of suffering and the desire to be joy-
ful are altogether natural. All animals, each as it can, bend every
effort to avoid suffering and to attain well-being. All animal
species, down to the most minuscule, seek to avoid suffering and
to find well-being, and it is in this manner that each one goes forward in its struggle for survival.

When the Buddhist teachings mention "all animate beings,"
clearly they mean all beings who reject suffering and desire pleasure. Meanwhile, the ability to discern good and evil is far greater
in human beings than in other animals. I think this is why, in
human society, where spiritual discernment has the most power,
religious faith has come to light. Visions, philosophies, and spiritual theories are all born in human society.

The human being's power of discernment is aided by our many
technologies and sciences, but it is because of our wish to be happy
and not to suffer that our discernment is actually used. However,
each time this discernment is employed, its very use creates a mul-
titude of problems and sufferings.

The other animals are surely affected by discernment. But the
human being alone will think not only of the happiness or suffering of the present moment but also of what will be in the future.
Because so much depends on our discernment, we think a great
deal about their future, and long stories of the past never fail to
occupy our minds. Other animals do not have this power. This is
why we, unlike the other animals, have so many hopes and so
many apprehensions.

I speak here only of what everyone can see on this planet. I say
nothing of the gods, the dragons, and the perfume eaters.[1] With the

three worlds, the six classes of beings, or the four births[2] of which the Buddhist texts speak, things expand even more. There are many other beings, all endowed with the ability to discern. In brief, human discernment is a good thing and very powerful, but always ready to secure us a little more suffering.

When animals have a full belly and a temperature that suits them, they relax and become tranquil. We human beings have all external circumstances favorable to us, but by the very fact of our hopes and our apprehensions, we often find ourselves in the greatest displeasure. Each time human discernment ought to intervene, albeit differently for each of us, we see again that our malaise is most intense, and hopes and apprehensions are most abundant. But this is not all. On this planet the most destructive being, all things considered, is the human being. One could almost say that if the human being did not exist, there would be much more peace and the environment would be better off.

If the human being did not exist, the fish and the innumerable other animals sensible to pleasure and pain would not suffer being exploited by humans. For those who exploit animals, animal life does not have the same value as human life. If the human being did not exist, some claim, there would be far fewer animals—without the human being, animals would only eat each other up! But would this not be a sort of natural equilibrium? If we think about it, would it not be better to desire the disappearance of the human being?

And yet all living beings, of whatever kind, love one another. So human beings love one another and can have concern for others. Our concern comes from our power of discerning, which is how we can develop our sense of compassion. But is it only the human being who has this capability? Among all animals, unselfishness, limited as it may be, brings benefits. Among the social animals, however, infinite compassion is the prerogative of the human being alone. A beast would have great difficulty surrendering to it.

Or we can approach the matter from the other end. Life, our very existence, is not dedicated to destruction. Could our whole life be reduced to an existence dedicated to destruction? Not at all! We do not exist to destroy, any more than we exist to suffer! Then do you not find that whether our lives are constructive or destructive lies in our own hands?

If we could be gifted with true discernment, and we could surround ourselves with loyal friends, we would have a life of great meaning: it would be constructive. It is important for us, then, to reform our mind by examining it in great detail. We ought to develop its goodness and its usefulness by reducing its harmful aspects. Is that not the essential?

To be sure, one could ask what we mean by "good" and "bad." Suffering designates something "bad," something undesirable. Suffering is a source of unpleasantness. It is happiness that we desire; happiness, then, will be our "good." We distinguish good and bad effects, those that are pleasant and those that are not, by considering their respective results. "Bad" is the cause of suffering, and "good" is the cause of well-being and what is authentically useful. When we have reformed our mind, our negative thoughts will diminish and our positive thoughts will increase. Then, we will suffer less and less of the "bad," and grow more and more in the "good."

Whether we have a religious belief or not, none of us wish to suffer. We all wish only to be happy. We ought to admire the positive qualities of our mind, then, and recognize its shortcomings for what they are. This is a very important point.

We are all alike: human beings are without any basic difference. We have different cultures, different religious beliefs; we are of different races; our lifestyles are different, as are our family backgrounds. But whether we have received an education or not, whether we are poor or rich, we all have the same potential, a potential for good as for evil. It is extremely important to recognize the existence of our negative potential just as much as that of our positive potential.

Peace of Mind and Happiness

[In the following paragraph the Dalai Lama refers to a meeting he had with this group several years prior.]

Several years have passed since our first instruction. Time always flies. It never stops. No power, no force can arrest the movement of time. What are we to do? We alone are responsible for using our time well or poorly. So let each of us reflect. If we have a sense of not having wasted our time, the only thing to do is rejoice. But if things have been very difficult, if we have been constantly busy, we wonder what all of that was good for and whether it was really necessary. Then we think of all this time that has flown. Do you not find that strange?

Becoming rich and famous: is that really the essential goal of human life? Money is important. A "name" is generally useful as well. But among those who have money, a name, and possessions— say, great wealth—we have seen more than one drowning in troubles and concerns. Others, by contrast, have neither name nor renown, they seem truly unfortunate from the material standpoint, but their minds seem at ease. Some have no money problems but are always having to take medicine. Yet others, even in the absence of all material comfort, feel physically well without having to take medicine.

What is their secret? When peace reigns in the mind, one is always happy, even if external conditions are not ideal. The body can gain health, but without peace of mind no happiness is possible, not even under the best conditions.

Then where is this secret? It is in our peace of mind. Would peace of mind come once one has wished for it? This would be very unlikely. The mere wish to know peace of mind cannot secure that peace. You know that one does not acquire money simply by wishing for it. One has to work to obtain it. Just so, peace is a possession of the mind, and this possession, this wealth, is not obtained simply by desiring it. Go to a big store in Paris, or even in New York. No one will sell you peace of mind.

Certain religious communities claim that their religions enable one to reach peace of mind instantly. But how could that be? I only know what I have studied, of course, but when I am told that it is possible to reach a certain peace of mind in no time at all, I become skeptical. It would be like asking your physician for an injection of peace of mind. I think the doctor would burst out laughing.

When your mind is encumbered with thoughts, and you are a perpetual "sad sack," you may think the only thing to do is to take some medicine—something that will keep you from thinking on your own and even make you a little foolish. But this treatment would be unsuccessful. A perfectly clear and totally at ease mind is one in possession of its capacity to discern good and evil, and this is something that would be hard to get by using medicine.

Analytical Meditation

It is only by training the mind that one reaches peace of mind. What training? I believe that analytical meditation, not just the meditation of concentration, is the best. An examination of our strong points and our shortcomings will produce in our mind a gradual change of attitude.

Sickness, for example, old age, and death—ours and those of our friends—are causes of suffering. They are too bad, of course, but just how bad depends so much on our state of mind. Let us take death. If, for you, death is impossible or unacceptable, then when you die it will be an unbearable experience. But once we admit that death, too, is part of life, that it is not impossible, that it is a component of life itself, things go much better when the moment actually comes.

In order to think about this a bit more precisely, let us attempt to pay close attention to emotions like hatred, jealousy, or craving that lurk in our mind: the instant these thoughts arise we experience a certain disquietude. By contrast, the moment we have thoughts of love, tenderness, and tolerance, we feel full of courage and strong in mind and spirit.

What is the use of this kind of observation? What harm could it do us? Just as we have extensively examined the outer material world, it is important that we examine the various states of our interior mind. This is the kind of exercise that I call analytical meditation: that is, the best way of training the mind to realize inner peace, a calm—something that concerns humanity as a whole, believers and nonbelievers.

Religious Belief and Conversion

When human beings are confronted with a serious problem, when they are deprived of their ability to cope, when they are desperate and abandoned, faith is a succor to them. It restores their hope. There are many religious systems on this planet, many incompatible views and philosophical systems that nonetheless are one in this; they all have their usefulness and correspond to people's different constitutions and aspirations.

Later we can discuss interreligious dialogue, but for the moment we speak only of Buddhism. I am always somewhat hesitant in explaining Buddhism to people who are not Buddhists by ancestral descent and who do not live in traditionally Buddhist lands. Generally it is better to follow the religious tradition of one's forebears; this brings more solid results. When we change religion, we may never adapt. Then, achieving results neither in the new belief nor in the old, we find ourselves in the clutches of a double contradiction. Respect for ancestral traditions is a guarantee of stability. But of course, in certain cases, a change of religion can be a most favorable event.

In Tibet, for example, practically everyone is Buddhist. Still, over the course of three or four centuries, certain Tibetans have become Muslims. Similarly, throughout the twentieth century, others have become Christians. In the Judeo-Christian countries, where Christianity is preponderant, we observe a kind of reawakening of attraction to Buddhism. If, then, after a precise examination of the situation and mature reflection, we think that Buddhism is suitable, that it corresponds to our individual aspirations, then there is nothing inappropriate in practicing Buddhism. This is even more true if one has never had a religious belief. If one feels an affinity for the explanations of the Buddhists, one need only study them.

Nevertheless, just because a particular individual has seen how suitable the Buddhist approach is for him or her, it is absolutely wrong for that person to criticize the religion of his or her ancestors, whatever it may be. This should be avoided. You who are here today then, reflect. If you decide for Buddhism, the situation is special. But in no case shall I become the advocate of Buddhism.

Conversion is not generally good in and of itself. It is often a source of conflict. In Mongolia there seem to be Christians engaged in "converting" people. I have looked into the matter and have not seen anything good there. And if I cannot appreciate the conversions effected by these Christians among Buddhists, then I also say that it is unsuitable for Buddhists to effect this kind of conversion in Christian countries.

On the individual level, matters are different. To be sure, Buddhism is what is best for me, for example; but that does not mean that Buddhism is best for everyone. For the practicing Christian, the best thing is Christianity; but that does not mean that Christianity is best for everyone.

It is nonetheless essential to know about all the different religions. On the one hand, such knowledge opens the mind and removes the risks of fanaticism. On the other hand, when, in one's individual practice, one incorporates the most adapted techniques of the other religious traditions, it becomes possible to practice a kind of mutual study.

THE ORIGIN OF THE DHARMA

Here, now, is how I am accustomed to explain the origin of the Dharma.

It was in the sacred city of Benares[3] that the Instructor filled with goodness, expert in skillful methods, and overflowing with great compassion preached the Dharma for the first time. He set the wheel of the Dharma turning and taught the Four Noble Truths to the Five Good Ascetics.[4] And so Buddhism began.

As you all know, the usual explanation is that there are two vehicles of Buddhism, the Lesser and the Greater, that is, the Vehicle of the Hearers and the eremitic buddhas [Hinayana] and the Vehicle of the Bodhisattvas [Mahayana]. The Greater Vehicle is in turn divided into the Greater Vehicle of the Sutras and the Greater Vehicle of the Tantras. The system of the Four Noble Truths, which forms all Buddhists' basic belief structure, necessarily follows this division into two vehicles.

The practice of the way as it is taught in the texts of the Lesser Vehicle constitutes the foundation of the Buddha's teachings. Without this foundation, it would have been very difficult for a "greater" vehicle to appear. When, within Buddhism, adepts of the Greater Vehicle judge a teaching inferior because it belongs to the Lesser Vehicle, or adepts of the Lesser Vehicle doubt that the Greater Vehicle really flows from the Buddha, they are making these judgements out of Buddhism's essence, and this is a serious shortcoming. Without the practices associated with the Four Noble Truths, or the way of the thirty-seven aids of the Awakening taught in the texts of the Lesser Vehicle, it is impossible to truly practice the spirit of Awakening of the Greater Vehicle, which is benevolence and compassion. I mean great compassion.

The same prejudices have occurred in Tibet between the Greater Vehicle of the Tantras and the Greater Vehicle of the Transcendences [the six transcendent virtues]. The adepts of the transcendent virtues did not look favorably upon the tantras. For their part, the adepts of the tantras had scarcely any respect for the Vehicle of the Transcendences, especially where discipline was concerned. This prejudice was a defect and an error.

The levels of the vehicles are, then, Lesser Vehicle, Greater Vehicle of the Transcendences, and Greater Vehicle of the Tantras. The fruit of the more humble vehicles is easily attained by following their practices. Nevertheless it is impossible, without mastery of these "lower" practices, to reach the fruit of the higher vehicles. Why? Because these lesser vehicles are the foundations upon which the greater take form. Among the teachings of the Buddha that have been preserved in all their integrity in Tibet, the Land of Snows, we find the practices of the Lesser and the Greater Vehicles, including the aggregate of the tantras. For me, this is an important fact.

The Three Cycles of the Buddha's Teachings

In the philosophical systems of the Greater Vehicle, what was taught by the Buddha in the texts of the Lesser Vehicle advances in breadth and depth. For example, the texts of the Lesser Vehicle concern only our Instructor Shakyamuni. In the first part of his life, he is said to have been an ordinary person and bodhisattva. Then, it is said, on the Diamond Throne [in Bodh Gaya, India], he undertook the way of juncture;[5] and he became an authentic and perfect buddha as he emerged from this diamondlike contemplation,[6] or way of cessation. These texts teach that it was only during the second part of his life that he was a buddha. However this may be, here it is a matter simply of what is called a supreme body of apparition,[7] not other bodies of the Buddha. In the Greater Vehicle, the system of three or four bodies of the Buddha prevails.

In the Greater Vehicle of the Transcendences, the Buddha will teach the system of the four bodies. He will explain how the four bodies are realized in the tantras. Likewise, when he teaches the different ways or paths, and the meditations proper to each one, the Buddha does not limit himself to the way of the thirty-seven aids of the Awakening, and especially not to the way of the nonexistence of the individual self.[8]

When the moment of the Greater Vehicle had come, the cycle of universal insubstantiality[9] acquired its breadth. All the theories, such as the system of the ten earths,[10] have constantly broadened since then. In the Vehicle of the Transcendences, the Buddha taught the practice of the six transcendent virtues and declared that the way was to be followed by combining method and knowledge itself.[11] In the tantras an eminently sublime thing is taught: the extraordinary union of practice and knowledge.

And so, once he had deepened[12] and broadened his teachings on the Four Noble Truths, the Buddha turned the wheel of the intermediate Dharma, that of the Greater Vehicle,[13] on the peak of the Voutours. He then pronounced the sutras of Transcendent Knowledge.[14] In these sutras the Buddha minutely studies the noble truth of the cessation of suffering that he had taught with the other three truths at Benares. In the third cycle of his teachings, he taught a variety of sutras that, like the principal sutras explicit in Continuity Unexcelled,[15] such as the *Sutra of the Potential of the Buddha*,[16] deal exclusively with the clear natural light of the mind.[17]

In a word, it was fitting that, with a view to ultimate intellectual comprehension, the truth of the way, otherwise known as the sublime wisdom,[18] be manifested. From then on the mind could attain to an ultimate state absolutely free of the two veils. And at the moment of the last cycle of teachings, when he pronounced texts like the principal sutras on which Continuity Unexcelled is founded, the Buddha taught the ultimate point of the clear light as the nature of the mind. This is the real sense of this kind of text, although certain sutras of the last cycle use a different language.

What the Buddha had first taught was found here more clearly and more profoundly. Later, in the Greater Vehicle of the Tantras, he taught extraordinary things such as the living practice of the "clear natural light of the mind." Indeed, this was the occasion on which he taught these things in their ultimate depth and immensity. Were not the deepening and broadening of what he had taught at the beginning only a natural sumptuousness and refinement? No. If the Buddha had restricted himself to his first teachings, he would have committed an error and his teachings would have gone against logic.

I repeat: the later teachings of the Buddha are more profound and clearer than the first. Were not these "deepenings" and clarifications only manners of digression? A luxury that would not be indispensable? I think not, for the teachings of the Buddha cannot ever be reduced to his first teachings.

Teachings of Provisional and Definitive Meaning

The Lord Buddha, our guide, the Lion of the Shakyas,[19] remained at the royal palace until age twenty-nine. Next, he practiced asceticism for six years. Then, at about thirty-six years old, he awakened to authentic, perfect buddhahood. For the forty years that followed his Awakening, he worked for the good of others. He had prepared the cause of all these events by accumulating merits and wisdom over the course of three great kalpas beyond measure.[20] During this long period of time, a causality developed whose effect lasted a mere forty years. Is this not out of proportion? This causality, a vast accumulation [of merits and wisdom], had only a brief effect and did not produce any other enjoyment.

Now the arhat state of the Hearers, the arhat state of the eremitic buddhas, and the buddha state are the three sublime states to be attained. Leaving out the time that the accumulations will call for, if one practices the thirty-seven aids to the Awakening that constitute the way leading to these three states, one necessarily follows the same way of principal meditation. How would the same cause produce three different effects? It is a rather vexing question.

If we posit that in the Awakenings of the Hearers and of the eremitic buddhas only the emotional veil has been eliminated, while in the Great Awakening the darkness of nonemotional ignorance has also been entirely dissipated, are we not making a distinction between a sublime fruit and two inferior fruits? Their cause is reducible to the thirty-seven aids of the Awakening, and even with the accumulation of merits and wisdom throughout three lives—one hundred kalpas or three great kalpas beyond measure—the realization of the result is not an effect of the mere duration necessary to realize the accumulations. If the differences were not altogether dependent on the *depth* of the ways followed, it would indeed be vexing to posit more or less elevated results.

The Buddha gave many teachings on subtle and gross insubstantiality, which is the subject of the meditation of the Basket[21] of the bodhisattvas, or of the sutras of the Greater Vehicle. And he taught the generosity and vast numbers of practices detailed in the title of the method. So, as the result or fruit is more or less elevated, the ways are great or little.

Indeed, from the viewpoint of the Greater Vehicle of the Tantras, the way of the union of the methods and of knowledge—in which the methods support the knowledge and vice versa, as the Greater Vehicle of the Sutras teaches—is insufficient for a realization of the absolute body and the formal body. Why? Because the absolute body and the formal body of the resulting phase[22] have the same essence. That is why—as long as their complete effective cause, this ultimate cause, is not the inseparability of methods and knowledge—it is difficult, in pairing methods and a knowledge that are essentially different, to attain an inconceivable result, such as the absolute and formal bodies that are inseparable in essence. The objection comes to mind at once.

If the system of the four bodies is expounded in the texts of the Greater Vehicle, the immense way of the methods and of knowledge that permits a realization of these bodies is taught in the Adamantine Vehicle of the Secret Formulas.[23] This is the essential point of the inseparability of the methods and knowledge that is taught, and this teaching bestows an extraordinary reliability on the theory of the four bodies.

But then, it will be said, the Buddha's earlier and later teachings are contradictory. This is not so! We must note that, especially in the systems of the Greater Vehicle, the declarations of the Tathagata[24] must not all be taken literally, for they can be provisional or definitive. It is good to take the definitive declarations literally, but not the provisional ones.

Let us clarify. One does not judge the definitive or provisional character of a declaration of the Buddha on the basis of its mere formulation—the letter. It is essentially its meaning—its spirit—that must be considered. So we will give the name sutras of definitive meaning to the texts that show forth absolute reality. Those whose content must be interpreted will then be sutras of provisional meaning.

So what is meant by *definitive meaning* and *provisional meaning?* Relative truth and absolute truth, it is explained, obey respectively the provisional meaning and the definitive meaning. We regard the definitive meaning as absolute truth, and *absolute truth is the ultimate mode25 of everything*. This ultimate constitution, being absolute truth, is called thusness,[26] so that absolute truth designates the ultimate reality of everything, whatever it be. When one can no longer be drawn[27] anywhere else, one can speak of an absolute, an ultimate. Such is the definitive meaning of the words of the Buddha. So the designation "sutra of definitive meaning" will attach to the sutra that shows forth, before all else, this absolute truth.

Relative truth, and the texts of provisional meaning, present the wealth and variety of a thousand and one metamorphoses of a most brilliant appearance. Yet this is not to be confused with the ultimate mode of each thing. One can take these relative truths literally. The spirit of Awakening, for example, which is benevolence and compassion, or indeed karmic causality—all of this must be taken literally.

Nonetheless, all that is taught about the heart of relative appearance cannot be applied to the ultimate mode of each thing. One can take them literally, but this does not mean they have discerned the ultimate mode of a thing. They must be interpreted—hence the name *provisional*. The sutras pronounced on these principles are therefore the sutras of provisional meaning.

And so, based on the foundation of the first teachings, the subsequent teachings become clearer and broader. We now discover things more profound and more vast. This is the great sublimity of these texts. We cannot say that these teachings are eminently sublime simply because they differ from what already existed, but rather because they deepen and clarify. They are treated in all of their breadth, as we have seen.

Method and Knowledge

Let us now consider methods. The division into Greater and Lesser Vehicles, and within the Greater Vehicle into sutras and tantras, is a way of understanding the methods. In the Lesser Vehicle of the Hearers and eremitic buddhas, the principal practice of compassion is not without power, surely, but it demands only that one not harm others and that one be helpful to them. In the Greater Vehicle, by contrast, committing oneself to the realization of the happiness of all animate beings and the abolition of their sufferings, implies a desire for the omniscience necessary to accomplish this intent. So the differentiation into Greater and Lesser Vehicles only follows greatness or smallness of thought.

Let us move on to the difference between the sutras and the tantras. Scholars all have their own ways of expounding this difference, but it is essentially the differences between the various aspects of the way—methods of accomplishing buddhahood—that constitute this distinction.

From the standpoint of knowledge, at present we hear it explained that Buddhists have four philosophical systems. Just as thought broadens in terms of method, in terms of knowledge it goes deeper. For example, the four philosophical systems of Buddhism admit insubstantiality. Now, while this insubstantiality has the same sense in the minds of the Vaibhashikas and the Sautrantikas, this is not the case for the Madhyamikas and Chittamatrins. The latter do not restrict themselves to the insubstantiality of the individual but teach the insubstantiality of all phenomena.

The difference between the Madhyamikas and the Chittamatrins with regard to the insubstantiality of all phenomena is a subtle matter. And analytical reasoning enables us to recognize the depths attained by these two philosophical systems. But it is wrong to say that the Buddha has given only these latter teachings, which are far more profound than the former. Why? Because both the latter and the former flow from him. And since they have their common emanation from the Buddha, some cannot be better than the others.

Can one readily gain a certitude about these truths[28] by examining them rationally, without also rendering oneself vulnerable to objections arising from analytical reasoning? For example, defending the unreality of the individual self without speaking of the insubstantiality of things—or maintaining that everything really exists, that the subject and object are not empty, and that everything is real—this is something that reason can invalidate.

If certain theses are not invulnerable to the reasoning of higher systems, if they yield to logic, it will be necessary to *interpret* the text in which they appear—the words of the Buddha—and place them among the declarations of provisional meaning that he pronounced with a precise intention. The profound teachings [those describing universal emptiness], it is explained, are logical to the point that no reasoning can invalidate them.

In all the declarations of the Teacher, one can find many points of seeming or actual contradiction. Yet they have all been pronounced by the same Teacher. How can this be? The Teacher has adapted them to the different constitutions and aspirations of his disciples.[29] This being the case, I find it profitable to know with certitude that these full and disparate teachings are truly useful to a wide spectrum of constitutions and aspirations.

THE NECESSITY OF THE FOUR NOBLE TRUTHS

But let us come to an explanation of the system of the Four Noble Truths. We shall first have to define them, then show their importance, and finally practice them along the way they inspire. This is tantamount to saying that they must be understood from within. Now the differentiation into four truths obeys a deepening of our view. We shall analyze them, then, by seeking to see which proposition [in the very proclamation of the Four Noble Truths] is not invulnerable to reason and which will be proved by reasoning.

If I say that the Four Noble Truths are true because they have been formulated by the Buddha, I shall have the problem that we have just seen. One cannot decide that certain philosophical points taught by the Buddha are correct and others not. At this level, the distinction into correct and false can only result from analytical reasoning.

Then how should we proceed? If these "truths" were but artifices of thought, it would be impossible that some of these conceptual inventions would stand up to reasoning and others not. Still, we are not speaking of truths that absolutely do not exist, that are pure products of the imagination, mere words. Let us take an example. The thought that someone is there when no one is there is simply a conceptual invention, and no logic will invalidate or demonstrate the reality of this pure product of thought. At most, one can declare that one such invention of the mind is useful and another not at all. There are even psychological explanations of this.

Nevertheless, on the whole, conceptual inventions are all valid. But are they all necessary? Necessary things actually exist, and can be proved by reasoning. But they must respond to a necessity. When, for example, we visualize ourselves as a deity,[30] our ordinary aspect is not divinized. To take oneself for a god is a mental distortion; still, it is necessary when we "practice a deity." In that case it is hardly a fixation on a god but a meditation oriented toward a deity. It is indeed a kind of conceptual creation, but it answers a necessity.

In the same way, when one practices recollection on the foul,[31] it is not a matter, in seeing all of the foul, of surrendering entirely to the foul as the ordinary world defines it. On the contrary, this meditation is the antidote [remedy or counteracting element] to desire and attachment: it proceeds from this necessity. So there are all sorts of possible situations.

I want to insist on this point. Logic invalidates all that does not exist in reality and is but a mental creation. Actually, when one takes an unreal object for a reality, the reality is vulnerable to reasoning. And what is explained on the basis of this reality must be sought by reasoning on the real existence of the object in question. Because this object is invalidated, it is impossible that anything at all really exists on the basis of this object.

So logic invalidates theories founded on the thesis of real existence. What do we mean when we speak of irrefutability by reasoning? We mean something that actually is, something fundamental that must be known as it is, something that logic cannot refute. Not to know how something is that is—this is what can produce useless concepts that do not stand up to reasoning. It is important, then, to establish the real mode [absolute truth] of every object. Knowledge of this real mode forms the basis on which one can explain what ought to be adopted and reject by reference to this object what should not be adopted.[32]

Then let us come to the Four Noble Truths taught by the Buddha. Suffering is something we do not want, and it must be repelled. To eliminate suffering, one must eliminate its cause. Once this cause is eliminated, one is necessarily delivered from suffering. This is surely how things should be explained, and I have no doubt about it.

If, then, we wonder whether it is possible to eliminate the origin of suffering, we must delve more deeply—think with more depth. In order to know with certitude what we should accept and reject, it is important to know the real nature of the cause of suffering.

The Two Fundamental Truths

We don't need to know the system of the two fundamental truths in order to comprehend the general theory of the Four Noble Truths. Nevertheless, to know the system of the Four Noble Truths so as to modify one's mind and gain a true certitude, it will be good to understand the theory of the two truths, which the majority of Indian non-Buddhists[33] also believe.

Among Buddhists, all schools, beginning with the Vaibhashikas, hold that there are two levels of truth. Still, concerning the essential points of the practice of the two truths, we shall refer in a general way to the philosophical systems of the Greater Vehicle, and in particular to the texts of the Middle Way.

Among the texts of the Middle Way, the theory of the two truths defended by Nagarjuna and his spiritual descendants Buddhapalita, Chandrakirti, and Shantideva proves very profound. It will be necessary, then, to understand the fundamental state of things on the basis of the explanation of these two truths as they are expounded by the sublime bodhisattva Nagarjuna and his heirs.

In order to explain the two truths, we must add the word *fundamental*. The two truths, which describe the fundamental real state of things, are not creations of the karma of ordinary beings, or discoveries subsequent to buddhahood, but something that one bears within.

In the context of the provisional and definitive meanings of the declarations of the Buddha, we have seen that the texts of definitive meaning express absolute truth, emptiness, and that the texts of provisional meaning concern relative truth. How, then, are we to define the two truths? Theories limited to the functions that operate on the mere level of appearances do not permit analysis to attain their durable situation, or their real mode.

On the level of mere appearances, one finds a variety of objects—in brief, the whole spectrum of perceptions designating the objects of the six senses,[34] that is, forms, sounds, smells, tastes, textures, and intelligible phenomena. Nor is it a matter of something one finds by looking for it when one is unsatisfied by mere appearance. Under the aspect of mere appearances, we distinguish an ultimate situation and a temporary situation. The temporary situation is the apparent temporary, or conventional, mode: what the mind finds there is qualified as relative truth.

Now, when one has studied, or sought, what might be the durable, absolute situation, or the *essence* of all of this variety of things, without limiting oneself to their appearance—when, unsatisfied by mere appearances, one seeks their durable situation—what one finds is the ultimate meaning of each of these things. One speaks of "meaning found by analytical reasoning on the ultimate truth of phenomena." And so, what analytical reasoning on the ultimate discovers is nothing other than absolute truth, and what analytical reasoning on the conventional discovers is relative truth.

But why is it necessary to seek the ultimate situation of things? Why is this a point of such importance? Well, despite the huge variety of appearances, one generally believes in the reality of immediate appearances, and this belief can bring about one's own destruction.

However this may be, can our actual situation present so much disparity between what is real and what is apparent? If things appeared as they are, their apparent mode and their real mode would coincide at every instant. If there were no disparity between the apparent and the real, common experience would represent as true what is not true, in ignorance of the extent to which persons are led into error this way.

Common sense tells us that it is a lie to transform a thing into what it really is not. We must then maintain that the apparent and real modes of an object *do not* coincide. In this case, what would the phenomena presented to us as the objects of our six consciousnesses[35] really be? It is important to examine them well in order to see whether they really exist when they are offered to us.

Mistaken prejudices generally lead to nothing. Falsified consciousness believes that what is is not, and that what is not is, and this belief comes from the depths of the person. Not only has the falsified consciousness slighted itself but it is *distorted*. Now, the distorted consciousness cannot accomplish anything constructive, either in the Dharma or in the profane world. It is important, then, to establish the real mode of things. This quest for the real mode of the things that exist is the same as that undertaken at universities.[36]

Under the aegis of the Prasangika Chandrakirti, adepts of the Middle Way declare that nothing really is, that nothing has being in itself, that no phenomenon exists on its own. These declarations permit in various ways the suppression of the negative emotions.

One may read in *The Two Truths of the Middle Way*[37] the words of the Svatantrika master Jnanagarbha:

If things are as they appear,
It is unnecessary to analyze them.

You, down there: your various silhouettes appear the same way to me as our forms here must appear to you. Things are indeed as they appear to us. And as they appear to us, they obey their conventional mode. This, then, is the extent of their being on the conventional level. It is impossible to analyze them, but their objective existence appears as an existence imputed to a particular conventional designation that suits them. Things are as they appear, then, and it is unnecessary to analyze them.

This kind of objective existence of things as they appear is hardly a postulate flowing from the perception of a sound consciousness. Would it then be possible under another mode—an extraordinary one? No, says Jnanagarbha. Then, he continues, what appears to us really exists. What he is trying to say is that, when we consider that an object is as it appears, two possibilities present themselves: either the object is good and attractive, and the mind moves near and meets it, or it is repugnant, and the mind withdraws. When something good or bad appears that exists objectively, two movements are possible: approach to the desirable and retreat from the undesirable. For Jnanagarbha, there is no negative emotion here. These movements of the mind are not distortions.

For Buddhapalita and Chandrakirti, it is the very possibility of asserting that these appearances of objects really exist that is incorrect. Nothing, they say, appears to us as it actually is. What appears to us appears to exist objectively because we are accustomed to regard it so, but it is not as it appears. Objective existence, then, is manifested in the objects of our six consciousnesses, but these objects are scarcely as they appear. To be sure, we clearly see that they are there, but they are not actually as we perceive them.

Something good presents itself, we approach it; something bad, we withdraw from it. This itself, say the Prasangikas, is the irruption of the negative emotions, attachment and hatred. For the Svatantrikas and the lower systems, these movements of the mind are in accord with their objects, and this group sees no distorted consciousnesses or negative emotions here. Note that, on the conventional level, the negative emotions are classified as gross or sub-tle in terms of realities judged attractive or' repugnant. The Prasangikas' definition of the negative emotions permits one to identify the more subtle emotions. But then, how shall one decide that something exists or not, as it appears? For this, one must fol-low the reasoning of the Middle Way.

If the object is as it appears, it will surely have to be found at the end of a process of analytical reasoning. Whatever object of the six consciousnesses presents itself to the mind, it is perceived as if it existed objectively. If it is really as it appears, we shall necessari-ly find it when we look for it. If this search is unsuccessful, we shall have the proof that the object does not exist objectively. Reasoning will invalidate its objective existence by proving that it does not exist objectively. The mistake, then, will consist in perceiving the object as if it had an objective existence. For it is not thus that it actually exists. Once we know that things are not really as they appear, we only have to accustom ourselves to this recognition for the power of the subtle negative emotions to diminish.

The manner of establishing the real mode of phenomena, that is, their emptiness, will then be subtle or gross. It is a matter of something that goes ever deeper, and whose ultimate state, formu-lated in the texts of the Middle Way, absolutely cannot be invali-dated by reasoning. The very thing that reasoning proves when it comes to ultimate nature—this explanation of the truth of cessa-tion according to the Middle Way—is, then, what we must con-centrate on.

It would seem that the four philosophical systems of Buddhism are in agreement on the noble truth of cessation. In the Madhyamika, and more precisely the Prasangika, approach to this truth answers an extremely profound necessity. It is in terms of the differences of subtlety in philosophical vision, then, that one will likewise observe differences in subtlety when one proceeds to the identification of the negative emotions, which constitute the truth of the origin of suffering. If we can establish this difference among the negative emotions that are at the origin of suffering, the truth of suffering, too, will be subtle, or gross. The truth of cessation, which designates the exhaustion of suffering, and of the origin of suffering, considered in this way, will also be subtle or gross.

As the thesis of emptiness can be subtle or gross, when we come to know the principles of subtle emptiness we observe the differences of subtlety in the theses on emptiness, and in the manners of its perception. In terms of this essential point, there are various ways of defining the truth of cessation, which is the very essence of emptiness. Besides, the distorted perception of emptiness gives rise to a theory of the subtle negative emotions from which flows a subtle truth of suffering. So it is a difference of depth in the approach to emptiness that entails different manners of posing the principles of the Four Noble Truths.

Thus, in order to understand a detailed exposition of the Four Noble Truths, it is necessary to know with precision the system of the two fundamental truths. It is likewise necessary to know the subtle theory of the two truths.

Asanga's *Ornament of Perfect Realization*[38] addresses the instructions on the meditation of the spirit of Awakening. An explanation of the two truths is followed by the principles of the Four Noble Truths in relation to the two truths and, finally, the three refuges [the Buddha, the Dharma, and the Sangha (Community)] in relation to the Four Noble Truths. The relationship between the two fundamental truths and the Four Noble Truths, and that between the Four Noble Truths and the three refuges, is addressed in great detail in Chandrakirti's *Explication of the Stanzas of the Middle Way*.[39]

It is essential to remember when the two truths are being explained that these are not, properly speaking, teachings on what is suitable to adopt or reject. The two truths have been taught in order to establish the real mode of an object. To be sure, they are not unrelated to the teachings on what is suitable to adopt or reject, but their main function is to allow us to know the real mode of an object. I say "the real mode of an object" because there is not a single phenomenon that is not included in the system of the two truths. The Four Noble Truths, by contrast, are devoted to practice, and explain what is suitable to adopt or reject.

However this may be, it is necessary to establish the two truths in order to explain the things that are knowable on the basis of their real condition, for the purpose of reducing suffering and being freed from it.

Recognizing That We Can End Our Suffering

How are the Four Noble Truths produced? What one does not desire is suffering. What one desires is pleasure. The undesirable, suffering, depends on causes and conditions. The desirable, pleasure, also comes from causes and conditions. *Pleasure,* here, or *well-being,* designates not only pleasant sensations but a lasting happiness, freed from all suffering; but this happiness also depends on causes and circumstances.

Suffering is what we do not want and what we seek to eliminate. The causes and effects of suffering constitute an ensemble, and those of lasting happiness, since they are that which must be brought about, form another ensemble.

Asanga, protégé of Maitreya, proposes the following analogy. Let us say that the pains of a disease known to us represent the truth of the suffering; that the germs provide the truth of the origin of the suffering; that liberation from the disease thanks to the elimination of the germs represents the truth of cessation; and that, finally, the medicine providing for the defeat of the germs represents the truth of the way.

When we do not notice that we were sick in the first place, we cannot notice any longer being sick. One who suffers from a sickness must first have a consciousness of it. Some who are ill claim not to be, and it is absolutely impossible to make them take medicine. And so one must recognize that one is ill. And so, when he taught the Four Noble Truths, the Buddha declared that it was necessary to come to a consciousness of suffering.

Once the suffering is recognized, we tell ourselves that we want nothing of this illness and that we are truly miserable. Then we seek the cause of the illness, and in recognizing it understand that we have fallen ill for a certain reason, under certain circumstances, and that it can be treated. We may even tell ourselves that we shall soon recover.

Just so, the Buddha declared that it was necessary to eliminate the origin of suffering. Whatever the cause of the illness, it is the cause, or origin, of the suffering that must be eliminated. One may wonder whether it is possible to suppress the cause of suffering. But it is because he had seen that that was possible that the Buddha declared it was necessary to "bring about the cessation" of the cause.

Patients who wish to bring about the cessation of the germs that are infecting them will therefore begin by recognizing them. Once they have seen the possibility of having a treatment prescribed, they will be aware of the cure that awaits them at the termination of their disease. Then they will wish to bring about the cessation. And once they are convinced that, in exerting themselves on the way of cessation, they will reach complete healing, they will commence the treatment.

If the disease is incurable, it is not necessary to undergo any treatment. Once one sees that it is possible to be cured, one begins the treatment. Likewise, when one discerns the truth of cessation, one wishes to bring it about, and to make this possible, the Buddha declared that it was necessary to "meditate on the way."

It is in terms of the practice of the Four Noble Truths, then, that he declared that it was necessary

To recognize suffering.
To eliminate its origin.
To bring about its cessation.
To meditate on the way.

What Is the "Self"?

What is the person who must recognize suffering, eliminate its origin, and bring about the way like? This person who wishes to be happy and does not wish to suffer, this "I," this self, must be examined in all of his or her depth. What we call "I," the "self," or the "individual" is what survives from one life to another, to credit the texts of non-Buddhist Indians who consider that an entity or being must exist that has come from a former life into this one and will depart for the next. But when one perceives something that is *not* what comes from the previous life and will depart for the next life, one is obliged to posit a self, an "I," or a person different from the five aggregates. Certain adepts of the self (or *atman*), then, maintain that the self is different from the aggregates.

Accordingly, to limit ourselves to the framework of a single life, it is essentially in relationship to our aggregates that we say that we are young, adult, or old. A person may say: I was small—at least for my teachers, for example, or for those who cared for me; then I was young; I gradually traversed the stage of maturity; then my hair turned gray, then it was white, then I lost my teeth, and now I am all wrinkled. When I say, alluding to my old body, "I have grown old," it seems necessary for me to have had an "I" from the first instant of my life.

Certain champions of the self, then, explain that the self is different from the aggregates, and that something like an "I" exists from the first instant of life. To explain things in terms of current biological knowledge: we certainly know that the particles constituting the body change from moment to moment. From this standpoint, the aggregates are pure change. We must think, then, that if one has an "I" from the beginning of this life, it will inevitably be different from the aggregates. If an "I" exists that is different from the aggregates, when one has understood the five aggregates—in other words, the body and the mind—there will have to be something remaining once the body and the mind have been detached from each other. But since there is nothing else to be found, there are no aggregates apart from the self.

The self is different from the aggregates, we hear it explained. It is immutable and abiding, unique and independent. In this case, the "I" of childhood and the "I" of old age constitute something unclassifiable, traced on the movements of the aggregates and therefore of a changing nature. Consequently, all Buddhists agree that no such thing as this substantial, abiding, unique, and independent individual exists.

Questions and Answers I

■ ■ ■ ■

How does one know that the real and apparent modes truly coincide?
Someone perceiving the coincidence of the real and appearance can also
entertain illusions.

Intellectual analysis leads to a conclusion pursued in thought by
meditation. If this conclusion is not mistaken, and corresponds to
reality, then the more we meditate, the deeper the experience of
our sensory apparatus will go. There you have a general explanation. I think, then, that we must count not on ordinary consciousness but on wisdom to guide our reflection.[1]

Indeed, when we have reflected well on such a thing, and have
come to a conclusion not subject to modification by any other
reflection, we gradually increase our experience. We might then
experience a certain disquietude, a sense of contradiction. But that
will depend on the degree of perfection attained by the analysis. If
the analysis has truly been followed to its term, regardless of the
angle from which we envisage its conclusion, and regardless of the
object to which we apply this conclusion, we no longer can experience the least annoyance. Perhaps this is how we ought to think.

Generally speaking, existence and nonexistence have a value on the level of conventional truth, and what is conventionally true, we hear, cannot be refuted by a different conventional truth. Then is there at present another thought that could contradict the thought emerging from an individual conclusion? For if there were another thought that could provisionally contradict it, there would inevitably be a third to contradict the second. This is how we should look at things.

Belief in the self, for example, contradicts the thought that being-in-itself does not exist. The existence of being-in-itself, then, is absolutely inadmissible. One can still tell oneself that things really exist, on the pretext that we are bound to them by benefits and burdens—which they indeed present—and for other, analogous, reasons. Belief in the real existence of things, then, contradicts the thought that has concluded their unreality, but this is only provisional. After all, meditation on the thought that sees that things do not really exist can develop ad infinitum, while the prejudice according to which they really exist, examined from all viewpoints with the help of many reasonings, does not find many opinions to support it. If the conclusion we have reached is contradicted by a different truth, this truth will probably be refuted in turn. Conventional truth concerns what occurs in each mind–that which a particular consciousness perceives.

As for knowing whether a perception is correct, or authentic, that depends on yet another perception, which must not invalidate it. But will a particular conventional object presently accepted be refuted by another conventional truth? Will it be refuted by the reasoning that analyzes the ultimate state of the object? It will be necessary to decide on its existence by proceeding to these two types of analysis.

I and those like me, think according to our abilities and add to the analysis of which we are capable the conclusions of experienced, reliable scholars. This is how we must proceed: by comparing and associating their experience with our own. These people, as accomplished as they are scholarly, are not simply those we find reliable in a general way. In order to guide our analysis rightly, they must be reliable, scholarly, and accomplished in the precise domain of this analysis. For if they were expert in another domain, one would have the right to ask whether it is correct to refer to them in the case at hand.

Indeed, if we examine an object in light of the ideas of Nagarjuna and Aryadeva, it is only to the writings of Nagarjuna and Aryadeva scholars that we must compare our thought. For, however reliable the texts of Asanga and Vasubandhu are, for example, the matter at hand does not, properly speaking, relate to their domain.

When you speak of "apparent mode," of the relative truth of all phenomena, and of their "real mode," their absolute truth, what do you understand by "all phenomena"?

The numerous metamorphoses that contribute to the appearance of things. We can think that what arises not from multiplicity, but only from the aspect of a single foundation, belongs to the absolute level. As we have said, we must distinguish what reason finds at the conclusion of the analysis of the ultimate and what it finds at the conclusion of the analysis of the conventional.

Take these flowers. What we can say of their forms and colors, their primary and secondary causes, and so on—all of this relates to relative truth. If we methodically seek the *ultimate flower* of these flowers endowed with forms and colors, we can find nothing. Accordingly, nothing exists that is not relative. Would these flowers actually be something else? No. But then how do they exist? They do not have objective existence, but they exist from the coming together of certain conditions.

We do not perceive these flowers as "existing from the coming together of certain conditions." A flower is a flower "in itself." That the flower does not exist independently of absolutely everything else—that is its real mode. Finding the thought that theorizes without analyzing permits one to classify flowers in white, yellow, and so on. This relates to the apparent mode of relative truth. What do we find when we analyze a flower to know its real mode? We discover a flower without real existence; we discover the impossibility of finding any flower at all. And that regards its absolute truth.

How can we have relationships with others if we have no self?

As I have explained, we must begin by assuring ourselves of the self. No one has ever said that there is no self. You see, it is like the flowers we have just considered: When we say that the self, the substance, and the flower do not exist really, or by themselves, we simply wish to say that things are produced in interdependence.

The four philosophical systems of Buddhism—Vaibhashika, Sautrantika, Chittamatrin, and Madhyamika—were they created by Indian intellectuals, or were they taught by the Buddha?

In our days, at the university the name Buddha evokes a historic personage who did not officially teach the Greater Vehicle. The Greater Vehicle did not appear in his "complete works." And, because the Greater Vehicle scarcely appeared in the collections of the Triple Basket,[2] the Svatantrika Bhavaviveka boldly wonders, in his *Brazier of Logic*,[3] whether the discourses of the Greater Vehicle attributed to the Buddha have not been compiled by Maitreya, Manjughosha, and other bodhisattvas.

For the university, and especially for the Hearers of his

entourage, the Buddha set the wheel of teachings turning. The Hearers, then, are the principal depositories of his doctrine. Then the laity who had faith in the Teacher felt a certain discontent, the university continues. Gradually, and solely so that the laity could consolidate their spiritual practice, the Basket of the Bodhisattvas appeared. In this Basket it is clearly written that ordination is an excellent thing, but the professors still dispute whether the bodhisattvas are monks or not. So some of them go so far as to claim that the absolute body of the Buddha is an invention of the laity.

I believe that these things deserve reflection. What I have just said follows the "university opinion," according to which the Dharma was woven of the thread of historical evolution. The Buddha, in this opinion, would have begun by teaching in an extremely condensed manner. Later, the Indian intellectuals made additions, and these teachings continued to be amplified. But what is the purpose of those who make this claim? They are convinced that the Buddha is merely an ordinary person. And the noble declarations of this ordinary person were elaborated by his disciples until the Greater Vehicle progressed to the present point. So much for a historical analysis according to the university.

When you are a Buddhist, you wonder whether it is possible, from a very general viewpoint, to reach buddhahood. Are there such things as samsara and nirvana? Should one seek them? If samsara and nirvana exist, is it possible to eliminate the negative emotions? What does the individual who has eliminated his or her negative emotions have that we do not have? The essential thing is to know whether liberation[4] is possible. Here, I think, we have the real questions.

If we perceive the Buddha as an ordinary being, then we are actually much better instructed than he. If we represent the Buddha as a simple historical personage, we are forced to admit that Nagarjuna was better instructed than he. But we ourselves are better instructed than Nagarjuna. Most of us have computers. And so, with our superior knowledge and our intelligence, we ought not enter the school of the Buddha. These two ways of thinking turn out to be radically different.

I mean that, if we consider Buddhism from the sole standpoint of evolution, the Buddha is but a human being, albeit a very warm one, who taught something very simple. Later, Nagarjuna arrived, and on the basis of teachings of the Buddha, invented certain new ideas. Next came Asanga, then Chandrakirti, who did likewise. If this is how things really happened, then, as I have just said, we are much better equipped nowadays, enormously better, at least with regard to the university. We live in a far richer era. These, then, are the viewpoints that differ. The ultimate view is: Is there a *shunya*,[5] is there a nirvana, is there the possibility of eliminating all the emotions that afflict us, and all the ignorance? Here are the essential questions.

If it is possible to eliminate the emotions that afflict us, then people have done this. But naturally we cannot compare ourselves with them. Certain phenomena seem to us difficult to understand because we still lack spiritual experience. But there are other factors to consider. Those who speak to us of their liberation should have no reason to lie, and they inspire our trust. Nor should there be a contradiction among the various declarations by all those who deserve our trust concerning these hidden phenomena. In order to judge these facts, in certain domains we have recourse for the moment to the declarations of a third party. It is very complicated. I shall conclude this subject tomorrow, because it merits further explanation.

The Self and Karma

■ ■ ■ ■

NONVIOLENCE AND
INTERDEPENDENT PRODUCTION

I shall begin by repeating what I always say. All of the teachings of Buddhism can be reduced to two things: the practice of nonviolence and the philosophy of interdependent production.[1]

This philosophy begins with a rough understanding that is gradually refined to the point of knowledge of interdependent production in all its breadth. Interdependent production, on which all Buddhists are in agreement, denotes the production of manifold metamorphoses—that is, of the variety of effects, from the sole fact of the interaction of causes and circumstances. The Four Noble Truths and the two fundamental truths, of which we spoke yesterday, are therefore explained in terms of interdependent production.

The one who brings together the philosophy of interdependent production and the practice of nonviolence is the person, the self. The one who establishes the view of interdependent production and experiences its benefits and drawbacks is, once more, the self.

Likewise, the one who believes in nonviolence and puts it into practice is to be sought in terms of the self.

THESES CONCERNING THE SELF

Many in India before the Buddha had already pondered the question of the self, or *atman*. For certain Indian non-Buddhists, the self is a distinct entity from the aggregates. Now no Buddhist will ever admit the existence of a self of this kind. But within Buddhism itself there are numerous theses concerning the self. For certain branches of the Buddhist school of the Vaibhashikas, the aggregates constitute the substrate, or the basis, of the qualities of the self. Other Buddhist thinkers believe that the self has its substrate not in the five aggregates but in the aggregate of the consciousnesses alone—not in the sensory consciousnesses but in the mental consciousness only.[2]

For the adepts of Mind-Alone [the Chittamatrins],[3] who prefer the criterion of the scriptures to that of logical argument, once it is posited that the mental consciousness is the substrate of the self, it becomes impossible to put one's finger on a mental consciousness that is not sullied, so it is necessary to posit the existence of a "fundamental" consciousness,[4] external to the six psychosensory consciousnesses. Thus the Chittamatrins propose that this neutral fundamental consciousness constitutes the substrate of the qualities of the self. And so, besides the six psychosensory consciousnesses, or associations, the adherents of Mind-Alone postulate the existence of a fundamental consciousness and an emotional mental consciousness.[5]

The tantras as well distinguished eight consciousnesses.[6] See, for example, *The Diamond Necklace*,[7] the tantra that explains the *Guhyasamaja,* the *Assembly of Mysteries*.[8] Still, we must recall that the fundamental consciousness of the tantras is not the same as the fundamental consciousness as the Chittamatrins conceive it. In their Chittamatrin writings devoted to the eight consciousnesses, Asanga and his brother, Vasubandhu, describe the fundamental consciousness as a totally neutral entity, while in the tantras the fundamental consciousness is most often an intentional metaphor for the clear light, and thus it loses its neutral character and becomes essentially positive.

Now all these systems of thought demand that we find something or someone real when we seek the object that the word *individual*[9] denotes. In these systems of thought, one does not rest content with the appearance of things that would exist by essence, but one recognizes that something real must be found when one seeks the designated object, which comes down to admitting the existence of objective realities beyond appearances. In other words, each school of Buddhist thought will explain in its own way that the existence of an entity is twofold: nominal and concrete. It is nonetheless necessary that the real substrate, the designated object whose existence is purely nominal, also exist really, or by essence. In all these systems, then, nominal existence is also inherent in the object named.

In brief, I mean that, in each of these systems of thought, in which phenomena can exist as designations and as realities, there must be real things functioning as bases of designation for the things designated. Necessarily, then, the designation *individual* depends on an actual referent, a really existing substrate. Now, in identifying this substrate one must of course agree that it is a matter of the mental consciousness. And if we are not yet satisfied by this thesis, we shall propose that it is a matter of the fundamental consciousness.

In a word, all these systems refer to one or the other of these categories. And so, with the exception of the Madhyamikas-Prasangikas, all the systems of Buddhist thought admit the existence of an object, a reality whose essence is to exist, an individual that, indeed, has only nominal existence but that, when it is a matter of putting your finger on it, will be for some the mental consciousness and for the others the fundamental consciousness.

In their commentaries on the extraordinary thought of Nagarjuna, his close disciple Buddhapalita and the two Prasangika authors Chandrakirti and Shantideva cite the same passage from the sutras:

Just as one speaks of the chariot
In dependency on the ensemble of its parts,
So one speaks, in relative truth, of the animate being
In dependency on its aggregates.

In other words, *chariot* is but a designation attached to the ensemble of the elements that, conventionally, constitute what we call a chariot. Never does one find any chariot as such in one or another of its constituents, in its parts, its particles, its form, and so on.[10] Meanwhile, the Buddha teaches that, just as one calls chariot the ensemble of the elements that constitute it, the designations *self* and *individual* depend on the aggregates, or again on the body and the mind. This fact permits Buddhapalita to write:

Did things exist by essence, it would not be
Necessary to assign them dependent names.

This certainly proves that they do not exist by virtue of their essence. Let us repeat the words of the sutra:

One speaks, in relative truth, of the animate being
In dependency on its aggregates.

One "speaks," or "one fastens the designation," of "animate being." The individual, then, receives this name by virtue of its aggregates. The aggregates form the referent (of the word *individual*), or its "basis of designation." And the thing named, the name that one gives it on this basis, is the individual. There is a contradiction, then, between the referent and the name. The referent and the denomination contradict each other with regard to the same particular object.

How can this be? The thing named is as the agent, and the referent is as the act. In the case of the individual, the individual is the agent, and the aggregates forming the basis for the designation "individual" represent the action of this agent. In other words, the aggregates are the appropriation[11] and the individual is the one who appropriates.

Now the author of the act and the act itself are necessarily different things. Here is the mistake that consists in confusing the agent and the action, so that it becomes impossible to find the individual in its referent, the aggregates. And the individual will hardly be found any longer anywhere other than in the aggregates, or among the aggregates.

Not that individuals, persons, do not exist at all. It is impossible to deny the existence of "individuals." But how do they exist? Their existence does not flow from their essence; indeed it is limited to a simple designation by the sole power of the name.[12] What is more, if one finds nothing in searching for the object designated by the word *individual,* one finds nothing either when one seeks the aggregates that supply the basis to this designation.

Once this existence is admitted "without examination, in conformity with opinion, and by ignorance," or once this real existence seen by common sense is duly analyzed, there is nothing to be found. We are dealing with a purely conventional entity, whose existence satisfies common opinion in the absence of analysis.

What we are faced with, then, is a purely consensual existence—absolutely nothing objective. But nothing of what satisfies common sense necessarily exists. "Real" existence suits the common expression, but all of what suits the world does not necessarily exist on the absolute level.

The one who can find nothing in seeking what is called "I" or "person"—that individual who, without analyzing them, experiences pleasure and pain, that being who piles up the causes—his or her existence is undeniable! The individual is scarcely nonexistent but does not exist independently. If personhood is found in the aggregates, the individual will exist by essence. If we agree that the individual exists by essence, we will surely have to find him or her by searching in the aggregates. The individual does not exist by essence. Given the fact that the individual is no more than a name, it is no longer necessary to find that individual.

One will admit, then, that the individual is a conceptual designation founded on the aggregates. Of the five referent aggregates, the aggregate of the consciousnesses is the principal. The word *individual,* then, denotes the continuity of the consciousnesses of a particular person. Theses diverge on the number of consciousnesses, but none of them do more than address the gross aspects of consciousness.

THE CONSCIOUSNESS AND THE CLEAR LIGHT

In the Unsurpassable Tantras,[13] distinctions are drawn among the gross, subtle, and very subtle consciousnesses. The gross and subtle consciousnesses are adventitious—produced when the conditions necessary to their existence are united, they disappear when these conditions cease.

Let us take the visual consciousness. It is produced when the condition "object," in this case an exterior form, as well as the dominant condition, the immediate condition, and the principal-cause condition, are all united. When these four conditions cease, the visual consciousness is extinguished. When, for example, the consciousness that perceives these flowers is extinguished, consciousnesses without perception of objects, and various other consciousnesses, occupy the mind. These consciousnesses are gross: they appear with the coincidence of conditions and disappear when the conditions are no longer.

Just so, the subtle consciousnesses, of the type of negative emotions or discursive thoughts, such as the eighty "indicative thoughts,"[14] appear when conditions are united and disappear when they are no longer. Under this aspect, they are also given the name momentary consciousnesses.

As for the very subtle consciousnesses, there are four of them in the system of the *Guhyasamaja*: empty, very empty, greatly empty, and all empty. The first three empties are "momentary"; only the fourth is "original." This all empty does not result from momentary conditions. It is not like the other empty-consciousnesses, which are manifested by the fact of the consciousness of certain momentary conditions and disappear with the disappearance of the conditions.

What is called the clear natural light subsists from all time. The gross and subtle consciousnesses all emerge from the absolute dimension of the clear light, and they all are extinguished in the dimension of the clear light. And so, when the clear light of the instant of death is manifested, there remains but the sole and unique clear light.

Once the six consciousnesses have been extinguished—in a word, once the warmth of the body as well as vision, hearing, and other sensory faculties are enfeebled—visual awareness and the other consciousnesses are extinguished. The gross thoughts disappear gradually with the enfeeblement of the brain. Finally, if all these consciousnesses encounter the right conditions, they will manifest themselves only if there exists a power, or habitual schemata,[15] permitting them to. There, we hear it explained, is the dimension of the clear light.

But then, is this natural spirit or mind a reality in itself? Does it exist by essence? The innate original clear light, too, presents itself as a succession of instants, and as such is undiscoverable. When a "clear light" is sought, nothing is found that would have real existing as its essence: the past instant exists no more, the future instant does not yet exist, and each second the present disappears. This very subtle consciousness is born and dies from instant to instant: its past instants are no longer, and the present instants are already destroying themselves.

However, the gross consciousnesses, from the perspective of their continuity, are the fluctuating creations of momentary conditions. The gross and subtle consciousnesses that dominate our life today, for example, all well up from the spirit of clear light particular to the instant of our conception. And they will all be extinguished in the clear light when it manifests itself at the moment of our death. And so the subtle and gross consciousnesses are momentary: when the old body ceases, all the gross consciousnesses that were founded on it cease also. And when one finds a new body, the consciousnesses founded on this body are likewise born. Extinction, manifestation, and so on obey momentary conditions.

As the innate original clear light is scarcely the creation of momentary conditions modifying the continuum, neither does it cease in dependence on the cessation of certain momentary conditions: it forms an uninterrupted wave. Consequently, among the instantaneous consciousnesses that are but experiences of knowledge and clarity,[16] the majority exist only in terms of the union of momentary conditions.

So, for example, it is by interacting with a material entity like the human brain that human consciousness is born. Not only must this awareness be linked to a human body in order to be produced; but, without the support of a human body, it could not be produced. Did you not know this? However, if the human body is the union of the conditions acting as support for this experience of knowledge and clarity, that experience results from the clear light. In the absence of the clear light, nothing could be produced by way of an experience of knowledge and clarity.

Again, this general mode of functioning can be justified as follows. What is not consciousness cannot be the cause of consciousness. It is simply impossible. Consciousness is not a composed phenomenon. Given the fact that, from instant to instant, it comes into being and falls back into nothingness, consciousness necessarily has a cause. In an instant of visual consciousness, for example, the dominant condition, that is, the organ of sight, will act as immediate condition. But this condition needs an efficient cause. No consciousness can be produced without an efficient cause of the same kind.

This is why the principal efficient cause of the gross and subtle consciousnesses, these pure instants of knowledge and clarity, can only be the clear light. Customary schemata acquired in earlier lives depend on the clear light to subsist. These flashes of knowledge and clarity are the deed of the pure light. But if we demand that the clear light itself be the product of another substantial cause, we commit the error of attributing to it a beginning. It would be perfectly absurd that the original clear light be the product of something.

What Buddhists call consciousness is not generally a phenomenon endowed with a form. It is nothing that would have a color, nothing grossly material. Consciousness is but an experience of knowledge and clarity. When we say that a phenomenon manifesting itself as a flash of consciousness and clarity must proceed from an efficient cause of the same nature, we mean that the efficient cause of consciousness is itself consciousness. In Buddhism, it is inconceivable that a material substance endowed with a form would be the efficient cause of a consciousness. It is very difficult, then, to admit that the clear light is produced in dependency on a gross substance.

What conclusion can we draw from all of this? That the innate original clear light is not the product of precarious instants of consciousness. On the contrary, it is the momentary instants of consciousness that spring from this original consciousness. The original cannot proceed from the momentary, nor can it proceed from external material phenomena, but neither does it lack cause. And it is because it does not lack cause that the clear light has no beginning.

The original clear light is not a creation of momentary conditions. There is nothing, then, that might prevent it from lasting. If it were a precarious phenomenon, whose existence depends on momentary conditions, these conditions would prevent it from lasting. I am not speaking here of an external antidote that would have this effect. Inasmuch as any momentary phenomenon depends on all the conditions that have preceded it, it will change aspects by the very fact that these conditions change.

Conditions do not endure forever; that is their nature. There is something that opposes their endurance. There is naturally a contrary condition or an obstacle that prevents the instant from enduring. What the momentary conditions have created is destroyed once these conditions cease. Now, from the very fact that the innate original clear light is not the creation of certain momentary conditions, we know that there is nothing that could prevent it from lasting. This is why it is said that the clear light has neither beginning nor end. And it is precisely this point that permits us to explain the succession of lives, commonly called reincarnation.

Since the innate original pure light is accompanied by impurities, it is an "ordinary being." Now, what is a "buddha"? When momentary constructions are all extinguished, or spoiled, in the dimension of the clear light, and when they no longer spring back up from it, then to remain constantly in the unique innate original clear light to be called a buddha.

The momentary phenomenon that is spoiled, or dissolved, in the dimension of the innate original clear light will not reemerge from it without reason. It is the energy of karma that prevents us from abiding in the dimension of the clear light: hence the necessity of familiarizing ourselves with the spiritual way. This is also why the "I," the individual, has neither beginning nor end—which does not militate against the "I," the individual, being found in a situation in which it depends on a gross body, and the gross body has a beginning and an end.

One must distinguish the gross body from the subtle body and from the very subtle body. Just as the consciousnesses, the gross and subtle body are momentary, and the very subtle body is original. The "container," or inanimate world on which the gross body depends, itself has a beginning and an end. And it is thus that we come to the theory of the big bang.

CAUSATION, KARMA, AND THE BIG BANG

For Buddhists, the big bang is not unique. One can even say that the big bang, too, is without a beginning or end. Certain physicists think that the big bang is unique and others that there is a multiplicity of them. How, then, would the "I," the individual, so designated in terms of the clear light, be the product of a big bang? The answer must be found in the truth of the origin of suffering. The innate original clear light, generally neutral, is the very place where samsara and nirvana separate.[17]

But then how does samsara exist? Because they cannot last in the innate original clear light, momentary consciousnesses, discursive thoughts, appear under the action of the karmic energy (or breath). The negative emotions follow. And they have the power to register[18] a portion of karma.

As we read in the *Treasury [of Scholasticism]*:[19] "Karma produces the variety of the worlds." And in the *Introduction to the Middle Way*:[20]

The uncontrolled mind produces
The negative emotions and karma,
The very matter of the inanimate worlds.

Consciousness, which is but a pure flash of knowledge and clarity, is anything but an effect of karma. It is produced thanks to its efficient cause, in conformity with its nature. The simple notion of the individual, for example, is not an effect of karma. In the individual, it is the fact of temporarily having a human body that is karmic. What flowers have in terms of the karmic is what their forms and their colors can provoke in pleasure and suffering. What only obeys the efficient cause that has just preceded does not depend on karma.

If we ascend, then, all the way to the cause of the material objects analogous to these flowers, we arrive at the "particles of space"[21] preceding the big bang, which are a residue of the preceding universe that has disintegrated.[22] I am unable to say whether the four elements [which constitute the material]—earth, water, fire, and air—also exist by virtue of karma. And it cannot be said really whether the temperature and the water necessary for these flowers depend on karma or not.

What do we call "karma"? Roughly speaking, *karma* designates causality, the chain of causes and effects, which proceeds from the nature of things.[23] The chain of causes and effects only obeys the nature of things: it has nothing particularly karmic. But what is most often understood by *karma* designates, within the law of causality, which remains general, the particular case of an action, or an effort, attached to a particular intention, which forms the cause of the corresponding effect and the power to produce it. We are dealing, then, in the general framework of the law of causality, with a creation attached to an intention, and it is in the context of this intention that we speak of good and bad acts.

In the *Seventy Stanzas on Emptiness,*[24] Nagarjuna writes:

To think that entities born of [certain] causes
In [certain] conditions really exist,
Is what the Instructor [the Buddha Shakyamuni] calls ignorance.
It is from [this ignorance] that the twelve elements[25] proceed.

In other words, the reality of what is nothing but a designation dependent on a cause subjected to certain conditions will scarcely be proved in absolute truth. *Ignorance* denotes the opinion according to which a simple designation would possess an absolute, or real, existence. Things whose existence depends on certain causes, in certain circumstances, exist not truly but only under certain conditions. If they are accorded true being, it is done in ignorance. And from ignorance to ignorance arise the twelve elements of interdependent production.

We have just described primordial ignorance. If we take as our basis the Prasangika tradition of the Middle Way, such as we have just seen it, primordial ignorance, which consists in this naive realism,[26] constitutes the first of the twelve elements.

It is from ignorance that attachment, hatred, and the other emotions that necessarily accompany realistic ignorance on a subtle level arise. For the Svatantrikas and the lower schools, it is a matter of movements of consciousness conformed to their objects. To say this does not militate against these appearances, which we perceive in such clear presentations, being admitted really to exist on the level of conventional truth by all schools save the Prasangikas.

Of all the former schools, for whom this conviction is a conventional belief and not a realistic demand, not a single one would declare, with the Prasangikas, that the subtle attachment and hatred of which we have just spoken are negative emotions. The object that they believe real inspires a withdrawal if it is not attractive. But if it is attractive, it will inspire desire, creating attachment. And when attachment to or hatred of the place of an object held for real have developed (to the point of being no longer subtle but manifest), all Buddhists are in agreement in recognizing, in this gross attachment and hatred, negative emotions.

The subtle attachment and hatred that accompany the realistic ignorance induced by subtle ignorance are not common negative emotions. This subtle attachment and hatred have the power to register good and bad karma, precisely the karma that gives existence to the samsara of subtle composition. The Svatantrikas and lower schools, however, do not agree that this is karma that forms samsara, since they do not hold subtle attachment and hatred to be negative emotions.

I think, then, that this subtle composition is able to found the twelve elements, gross as well as subtle, of interdependent production, beginning with the subtle consciousness that, at the moment of the cause, is inscribed as the habitual schemata (of a particular experience). This will be the explanation of the twelve elements of interdependent production, without our having to distinguish two series extending from ignorance to old age and death, of which the one would derive from the subtle negative emotions and the other from the gross negative emotions.

Questions and Answers II

■ ■ ■ ■

"The four philosophical systems of Buddhism—Vaibhashika, Sautrantika, Chittamatrin, and Madhyamika—have they been created by Indian intellectuals, or have they been taught by the Buddha?"

At this point I should like to finish answering yesterday's question of the "Way and Fruit." In Sakyapas,[1] there are four criteria of truth: the words of the Buddha, the great treatises, the spiritual master, and personal experience.[2]

Let us consider a teaching, then, and see how one can have an adequate consciousness of it in the natural order of things. Truth [for the Buddhist Sakyapa, of course] begins with a citation from the Buddha. It continues in the great treatises that resolve all the enigmas it raised. Once one is convinced of the truth drawn from the sutras and treatises, the criterion on which one must rely is the spiritual master, who, by his practice, has attained realization.[3] It is thanks to the master that, in the psychic continuum[4] of the disciple, the criterion of truth of personal experience will be able to operate.

If we evaluate these four criteria of true knowledge by the

measure of certitude it is possible to acquire, the criterion of personal experience will hold first place. When an individual really has a meditative experience, the conviction that he or she then acquires will not be fundamentally shaken by later moments of joy and of sorrow. All sorts of things can happen in life, among them some certitudes that secure a bit of happiness and some certitudes that enable an individual not to fear at the moment of death.

Are there not a thousand ways to consider things? It ought to be possible to live peaceably. Indeed, this is what happens with those who have the experience of even an inferior realization—not to mention the experiences bound up with the superior realizations, such as the realization of the view of emptiness or the manifestations of wisdom as transmitted in an initiation.[5]

Individuals who have had an authentic, though ordinary, meditative experience nevertheless rely on this criterion to think that they have had this experience in receiving the blessings of the master who instructs them. They then perceive the criterion of truth represented by the spiritual master. When the criterion of the master is a certitude, it is possible to see that this master has gained authentic realization in practicing along the way guaranteed by the great treatises. One is then obliged to observe that the scriptures that have inspired the master's practice are criteria of knowledge that do not deceive. So, in ascending all the way to the master of teachings, the Lord Buddha, one will agree that his words are criteria of true knowledge.

In comparison with the ordinary experiences we can have, the experiences of the great masters are eminently superior. We have, inevitably, hints of these experiences stored up in the histories, and, in the feeble flicker of our little ordinary experiences, we can understand that such experiences are possible.

For example, myself— I have no experience. In terms of years I am old, but as for experience of the Dharma, I am young indeed.

Still, when I think of things like the spirit of Awakening, love, and compassion, or, again, of the philosophy of emptiness, I wonder what this permits me to judge. Well, I dare to think that Nagarjuna is fundamental. Truly. I think that very sincerely. It is he who declares:

> To Gautama[6] I render homage,
> Who, having received me in his love,
> Teaches me the Dharma [of the] real,[7]
> That I may deliver myself from all the philosophies.[8]

Nagarjuna was as intelligent as he was learned, and the esteem that he nourished for the Buddha indicates two things: that he considered the Buddha a being who does not deceive, an infallible criterion of truth, and that he would never have considered him a simple, ordinary being full of goodness of soul, a good patriarch of the past. And, if we reflect well, we see that we do not at all regard our gracious Instructor in that fashion. Nagarjuna's knowledge all goes back to the words of the Buddha: in no way is it a matter of ideas that the Buddha had not emitted—in other words, of which he had not known—and that Nagarjuna had drawn from his own intelligence.

One might say, "In our day, we know many things that Nagarjuna did not know. We ought to be at least a little more 'knowledgeable' than he. So it would be very difficult for us to make him our master were it given to us to encounter him." For the majority of those who see things this way, the Buddha manifested himself in human form, grew old, and died. Still, if we truly reflect on the spiritual qualities of the Buddha, we can realize that this is not at all the case.

The Buddha has four bodies, according to a theory that Nagarjuna considers true because he himself has experienced it.

Likewise, the accomplished scholars of India and Tibet have directly tested its value. Does that not confirm the validity of this theory? Once we are convinced of its theoretical validity, we can understand it intellectually to the point of conceiving a certitude and admitting that the system of the four bodies of the Buddha established by these trustworthy sages is, beyond any doubt, true.

Therefore Nagarjuna declares:

To Gautama I render homage,
Who, having received me in his love,
Teaches me the Dharma [of the] real,
That I may deliver myself from all the philosophies.

So saying, he bows before the numberless and vast teachings the Buddha dispensed, in terms of the capacities and aspirations of his disciples, in order to scatter their mistaken views. This, then, is why we Buddhists believe that the four schools of Buddhist thought flow from the Buddha. To say that Buddhism has suffocated along the path of historical evolution is to stand with the view of modern historians. We Buddhists see things differently.

Do those who have become buddhas retain their individuality?

On the level of buddhahood, there exists an individual identity.[9] It is well that it exists—otherwise, what an inconvenience! There would be nothing pleasant in becoming a buddha if all the buddhas were melted into one.

If we are concerned only with the good of others, how shall we accomplish our own good?

In order to love, one must begin by loving oneself. It is necessary to have an example of love at the moment of loving the other. When we do not love ourselves, can we truly love someone else? Each of us can experience a great deal of love for an ordinary being. Certain people risk their lives for love of an idea. And others, out of compassion and for the good of others, come to disdain their own personal happiness. These last are always happy, even if they must practice restraint, even if they must suffer in their flesh. In general, then, when one is concerned with the good of others, one accomplishes, by the same token, one's own good.

Is there a collective karma that is heavier for certain peoples, such as for the Tibetans, the Armenians, the Jews, or the Gypsies?

I do not believe that all of these individuals have really accumulated karma together, at the same moment and in the same place. They have accumulated bad karma in different places and at different times. Then, at the hour of retribution,[10] they have experienced the maturation of what their karma has in common. At least this is what I think.

The training of the mind[11] frequently provokes problems, sufferings. What can one do either to avoid them or to resolve them?

We must compare long-term interests and short-term interests. As *Journey Toward the Awakening*[12] teaches in the chapter devoted to patience, in order to meditate we must have recourse to methods with competency. If we stubbornly adhere to one technique of meditation—let us say, when we pass all our days in analytical meditation, or on a reasoning that is always the same—there comes a moment when we not only tire but are forced to observe that we have not made one inch of progress.

That is when it is important to concentrate on all sorts of subjects. The subjects of meditation are but foods for the mind, and just as the human being is nourished by various foods, the mind does not turn away from the variety of tastes of what sustains it. In analytical meditation, we reflect on all sorts of subjects, which especially must not lose their freshness. By contrast, when one meditates in quietude,[13] one must hold to the object of concentration alone.

Do acts inevitably produce effects? Is there a way to avoid their consequences?

Every act, virtuous or injurious, can be eclipsed, so to speak, by another, more powerful act. One can purify oneself of a duly registered negative act by repenting of it and resolving not to reproduce it.[14] But a single instant of violent anger is capable of annulling the power of good retribution of a great number of virtuous acts.

Suffering and
the Origin of Suffering
■ ■ ■ ■

HABITUAL SCHEMATA AND IMPRINTS OF ACTS

The ignorance of naive realism consists in believing that things exist in themselves, and the twelve elements of interdependent production are all the issue of this ignorance about reality. Consciousness forms the third element of the series.

Once one has registered a bodily act, for example, once this act is accomplished, has one definitively finished with it? From the fact of this act, and at the precise instant at which it has taken place, the atmosphere has changed. When we quarrel, for example, and are moved by hatred, the atmosphere is immediately degraded. When the quarrel—the act—is over, its energy, we hear, leaves an imprint[1] in the consciousness. The Indian scholars have abundantly studied the terrain on which this imprint is deposited, and they explain that fundamental consciousness is, among other things, this terrain. They also explain that this terrain is twofold, like the schemata that are inscribed there and that can be temporary or lasting.

The terrain on which the temporary schemata are inscribed is nothing but immediate mental consciousness. As for the terrain on which the lasting schemata are inscribed, it will not be found in the "I" or individual as we have approached them. It will be found not, then, in what functions as referent to the very relative designation "individual" but in the simple "I," so named on the basis of its referent.[2] The continuity of this simple "I" is maintained from life to life: would the simple "I," so named with respect to the continuity of consciousness, be permanent? It is certainly the one that posits itself the habitual schemata. So it is said.

Let us take the example of a verbal act—good or bad, it matters little. Once it has ceased, it leaves an imprint—a future habitual schemata. Or rather, in the Prasangika texts, Nagarjuna himself explains that the composed phenomena can be concrete or abstract. And so, he says, as the concrete designates the act, the abstract is that which "remains from the act" once the act is abolished, for what remains of an act that is no longer is also a composed phenomenon. These two composed phenomena, explains Nagarjuna, have in common the production of a particular effect. Once the verbal action, for example, is no more, the continuity that is maintained after its disappearance exists perfectly well, and it is this continuity that, subsequently encountering certain conditions, will have the power to produce a particular effect. It is precisely this potential that becomes inscribed in the simple sensation of the "I."

At this juncture, let us take the example of the karma that provokes the existence of the aggregates of the subsequent life. When, finally, it encounters the necessary conditions, this karma has the power to permit the aggregates to exist. The imprint left by this act, or again, the "concrete abolished"—what subtly survives its disappearance—constitutes a real, or causal, power, from which flows "thirst," which is double and consists, on the one hand, of not wishing to suffer and, on the other hand, of wishing not to be deprived of happiness. Intensifying, the thirst releases the appropriation—the appropriation of the desirable, for example—and it is the intensity of the thirst and of the appropriation that, at the moment of death, calls for the element of becoming. There is nothing karmic here. *Becoming* is the name for the tenth element of interdependent production—the instant when, with the end of the karma of the life that is terminating, the power of attracting the subsequent rebirth has reached its full power.

Next come the elements birth and old age and death. In order for there to be rebirth, the preceding rebirth must have ceased with death. There is no intermediate existence, or bardo, between death and rebirth when rebirth occurs in a sphere of the Formless. In all other cases, there is a bardo, and I believe that it may be useful at this point to give a summary explanation of the existence of these bardos of death and of becoming.

DEATH, BIRTH, AND THE BARDOS

What happens at the moment of death? In order to answer this question, we shall adopt, wholesale, a tantric view.

All momentary consciousnesses, even appearance, increase, and near obtainment, are reabsorbed according to the process of gross dissolution.[3] In the end there remains only the pure light. This dissolution, which obeys karma and so is not the effect of a yogic practice, is called death. One speaks of the "clear light of the moment of death."

The process of dissolution designates the successive disappearance of the gross elements—earth, water, fire, and air—and of consciousness. Gross respiration ceases when the element air vanishes. Medicine holds that after exterior respiration ceases, the cerebral functions will not hold up for long. Still, when the air is "dissolved in consciousness," there remain four levels of dissolution: one must pass through the first instant of discriminating consciousness, the second, the third, and the fourth.[4] Still, if we hold to the texts, death is effective only at the cessation of the clear light of the moment of death.

As a general rule, one remains three days in the clear light. I speak of a dying person whose general state of health was balanced, and not of a moribund worn down by disease. But nothing is sure in this matter. Some remain there but a fleeting instant. By contrast, the individuals who seek it voluntarily, or those who know certain yogic practices, can remain in the clear light one, even two weeks. And so Ling Rinpoche[5] remained thirteen days in the clear light. In Dharamsala,[6] I have known people who remained there from one week to ten days. I have heard of a person in Lhasa, in Tibet, who is supposed to have remained there an entire month.

Whatever the case, it is said that, as long as the clear light lasts, neither the old body nor the bond between the support and the supported one[7] ceases. Because the bond that unites the body and the mind has not been broken, the body does not decay. Once the clear light ceases, this bond is broken. The clear light then detaches itself from the corpse, and the corpse begins to decompose.

Death necessarily has causes, and it arouses very particular perceptions. The causes of death are manifold, but they can be ranged in three groups: the death that occurs with the accomplishment of karma, the death that occurs with the exhaustion of merits, and the death that occurs because dangers have not been avoided.

The death that occurs when one has not taken care to eliminate momentary inauspicious conditions, then, has its cause in the fact of having succumbed to danger. Death by exhaustion of merits takes no account of possible longevity and occurs because all the conditions favorable to the continuation of life have not been completely united. As for death by accomplishment of karma, it occurs when the principal karma[8] is entirely accomplished, even if the necessary exterior conditions for the continuation of life are all united. The exhaustion of merits and accidents are generally owing to karma. Still, is death by accomplishment of the principal karma the same as the death that follows the pure and simple exhaustion of karma?

The psychic experiences particular to death are numerous. The *Treasury of Scholasticism* seizes upon the gross aspect of consciousness and explains that, at the moment of death, one can be found in a positive, negative, or neutral state of mind. The *Compendium of Scholasticism*[9] describes more subtle states of consciousness than does the *Treasury* but less subtle states than do the tantras, where there is mention of states of awareness much more subtle still. We then hear of a "subtle consciousness of the moment of death" with respect to the more gross states.

This subtle consciousness of the moment of death is strictly neutral, but the Tantras of the Unsurpassable Yoga explain that certain practices have the power to make it positive. Whatever the case, when the dissolutions are successively accomplished, all the way to proven death, an "I" suddenly arises, an "I" attached to the real existence of the individual, the sensation of oneself as no longer existing. And this is the sensation that initiates the bardo.

And so, once the clear light of death is extinguished, we have the bardo. In the bardo we have a subtle body, by comparison with this material body of flesh and blood that is ours at present. For beings whose form is subtle, distance does not matter. And from the very fact that one has a subtle body, one merely wishes something and it is realized. In this bardo, a cycle is accomplished every seven days.

The system of the bardos is peculiar to the tantras. True, the sutras subscribe to it as well, but they do not deal with it in detail, as do the tantras. The special body one has in the bardo is not unlike the body of a dream. I am speaking of the perception of the body not in ordinary dreams but in the yoga of the dream. Certain people can have special dreams when they awake from the karmic schemata that lend themselves to this perception. Others can even detach their dream bodies from their bodies of flesh.

It is generally explained that the special dream body is the product of the breath, or of a particular aspiration of the person meditating. On the level of the sutras, there are no practices especially centered on sleep and the dream, but in the Tantras of the Unsurpassable Yoga practices, or meditation techniques, of sleep, of the clear light, and of the dream are explained.[10]

There are four modes of birth: in a womb, from heat and humidity, from an egg, and by a miracle. We shall here envisage the bardo in terms of birth in a womb. The bardo comes to an end at the precise moment of conception. The texts specify that conception takes place when the father's sperm and the mother's egg unite during intercourse.

In our day we hear of "test tube babies." Conception, then, can follow a multiplicity of paths. We are witnessing the appearance of a new paradigm. I have heard it explained that it is possible to have little ones without a father, just from the cell of the mother, and so without the conjunction of the paternal seed. According to this theory [of cloning], it is going to be possible to manufacture human beings. I see nothing wrong with this. Birth has already, for thousands of years, depended on the meeting of the paternal seed and the maternal egg. One can even go back in time to the moment of the appearance of the first living being: at this precise instant, the distinction between father and mother had absolutely no currency. Only gradually was the mode of conception modified.

The *Sutra Imparted to Nanda upon Entry into the Womb*[11] explains that, once it has been conceived in a womb, the human being forms week by week until it has a viable body. Thus begins the element of interdependent production called birth. And it is explained that, from the first day of birth, suffering constantly grows. Accordingly, the old age aspect of the element old age and death cannot be limited to what we generally call old age. It designates rather the fact that, at the very instant when we were conceived in a womb, we embarked on the process of our aging.

THE SUFFERING OF IMPERMANENCE

The two final elements of the series, birth and old age and death, should be understood as the totality of the sufferings of a human life, beginning with the sufferings of old age, sickness, and death. Our life begins, then, with the element birth, and ends with the aspect death of the element old age and death. Between the two unfolds a rich package of sufferings, starting with aging, sickness, the vain quest for what one desires, and painful confrontation with what one in no way desires.

Suffering properly designated, which is called suffering of suffering, comprises the sufferings of birth, old age, sickness, and death. But then what is meant by "suffering of change"? Certainly not the painful sensation. Actually, the pleasant sensation itself. It is not rare, indeed, that a decreasing painful sensation is gradually replaced by a sensation of well-being. And, in a certain way, any pleasant sensation eventually degrades. Likewise, the perfections of this world, whatever they may be, all finally decline. So it is that what rises finally falls. What has been gathered is finally exhausted. Those who have assembled must scatter. All that is born will die.

And we still suffer when we possess what is best in this world. We can be celebrated and wealthy, for example, to the point of being blasé about it, or apathetic, which represents a source of torments. When we possess none of these perfections, of course we suffer from being deprived of them. And when we possess them, what distress at the idea that they are constantly deteriorating! All of this is nothing but suffering.

In our search for happiness, it is certainly for satisfaction that we do everything to be happy. We realize our desires in order to reach a certain contentment. Then, if we have "never enough" of it, as it is said, we could possess all the marvels of the world and they would never, absolutely never, bring us complete satisfaction. But to be unsatisfied is a suffering.

The third type of suffering is the suffering that steeps the conditioned world. This suffering of composition means that, given that birth is subject to karma and the negative emotions, there is nothing, and no one, that will not begin in suffering and end in suffering as well.

When all is said and done, true happiness simply does not exist. In view of this fact, the Buddha taught the Four Noble Truths and their sixteen subdivisions, beginning with the truth of suffering, whose four particularities are impermanence, the painful, inessentiality, and the emptiness of everything.

The impermanence of which the Buddha spoke, then, is not ordinary impermanence but subtle impermanence, the destruction that takes place from moment to moment. Every moment is annihilated in the following moment. There it is extinguished. It is not merely that the moment no longer exists once the following moment has supervened: the existing moment is being destroyed even as it lasts. But what produces it and makes it last? The moment is not destroyed when it lasts, or when it has ceased under the action of the following moment. The very cause of the production of the moment is the cause of its destruction. It is precisely when it exists that its cause produces it as a self-destructive entity unable to subsist. The moment, then, depends on a cause different from itself.

IGNORANCE AS THE CAUSE OF SUFFERING

Of the twelve elements of interdependent production, eleven issue exclusively from ignorance. They are, then, dependent on ignorance. When we hear of primordial ignorance, when it is explained that ignorance comes first and composition second, each element is being made the necessary condition of the following element. This does not mean that the end of an element signals the end of the following element. The antecedent elements produce the subsequent, and the subsequent depend on all the elements that precede them.

Ultimately, the circle of our existences, samsara, depends entirely on ignorance. Ignorance is a negative emotion. The word *ignorance* denotes any consciousness that secures a precise individual a negative emotion—an instance of malaise, or of something unpleasant.

To *Journey Toward the Awakening,* the veritable enemy consists of the negative emotions. While the ordinary enemy can become a friend, the interior enemy, the negative emotions, will never be able to do so. Therefore I find that life contains nothing pleasant, entirely subject as it is to the enemy negative emotions, which can do nothing but harm.

At the heart of the Four Noble Truths taught by the Buddha, the truth of suffering is the effect of the truth of the origin of suffering, which is its cause. I explained to you that the initial cause was ignorance of reality—that this ignorance had the power to produce the sufferings of birth, old age, sickness, and death, and that this was the truth of suffering. Is this actually the order that I followed?

Just as the Buddha taught that one must gain consciousness of the fact that one is sick, and suppress the cause of the sickness, so when we meditate we shall begin by thinking of suffering. When one thinks of suffering, one wishes that it would disappear. And when one wishes that suffering would disappear, one wishes to eliminate its cause. And so the Buddha first taught suffering. Only afterwards did he teach the origin of suffering.

It is only when, in thinking of suffering this way, we find ourselves miserable at the idea of depending on negative emotions that we begin to renounce, as we say—literally, to "wish to emerge from it." For the most part, we know, perhaps from experience, that it is possible to dampen these states that designate attachment and hatred. But is it possible to destroy the negative emotions to their root? Does a state exist in which one is totally freed from the negative emotions? This certainly calls for reflection. Which takes us to the truth of cessation.

THE TRUTH OF CESSATION

The truth of cessation denotes arrest, or cessation, with the help of an antidote. *Cessation*, then, is that which, with the help of an antidote, renders suffering and the negative emotions unfit to be born in the one who had not yet produced this antidote.

Cessation puts an end to suffering and its cause. How? With the help of an antidote. For every type of cause of suffering, a certain condition will be an antidote, which will prevent it from reproducing and will transform it into something unable to reproduce. *Cessation,* then, means the production of the antidote.

As we have seen, from a certain angle the essence of the mind is clear light, and when it is said that the innate original clear light is neutral, what is meant is that the knowing and clear nature of the mind remain forever immaculate. There are moments when the mind of clear light is accompanied by impurities. Since in certain conditions impurity is possible, we say simply that it has not been eliminated. As long as the clear light is manifest, the negative emotions cannot manifest themselves. A distorted consciousness is therefore added to the essential clear light of the mind. Realism is the idiocy in which the negative emotions take root: a distorted consciousness cannot rest on any criterion of true cognition.

When, in his *Unsurpassable Continuity,* Asanga writes that "impurities are momentary," he does not mean that they spring up from nothingness. They are "momentary" in the sense that, while they exist from time without beginning, it is always possible to disengage oneself from them. It is in the nature of the mind of clear light to be able to know objects, realizations, and the other qualities to be realized. The mind of clear light is naturally provided with all qualities, as Asanga explains. Its power to produce the qualities does not result from certain conditions but is inherent in it. Given that a powerful antidote exists to counter these conditions, which are momentary because it is always possible to disengage oneself from them, and given that impurities are momentary and the qualities are inherent [to the essence of the mind]—given all this, the Awakening, the truth of cessation, and so on are possible.

Do you think, after all that has just been said, that the truth of cessation is possible? When one attains to this truth, one is constantly happy. I am speaking not of pleasant sensations but of a situation of constant happiness.

Where, then, does the truth of cessation work? In the mind. The schools of Buddhist thought have posited different theses on the essence of this truth, and the Prasangikas explain that the truth of cessation is nothing other than absolute truth. Tibetan scholars, too, have posited contradictory theses on this subject. If one conforms to the thought emerging from the writings of Nagarjuna, the truth of cessation is not only absolute truth but also the most happy thing there is, when it is related to the nature of the mind.

Accordingly, in his *Fundamental Treatise,*[12] Nagarjuna says that "liberation is the deed of the exhaustion of karma and of the negative emotions." By this he means that *liberation* denotes the exhaustion of karma and of the negative emotions with the help of effective antidotes.

Then how does one undertake effectively to eliminate karma and the negative emotions?

Karma comes from the negative emotions, and the negative emotions are the effects of the thoughts of an incorrect mental activity. The thoughts of an incorrect mental activity, says Nagarjuna, result from the conceptual constructions of the realistic belief:

> Liberation is the deed of the exhaustion of karma and of the negative emotions.
> Karma and the negative emotions result from discursive thoughts.
> The discursive thoughts flow from the constructions of the concept.[13]

Karma and the negative emotions thus result from an incorrect mental activity: "Discursive thoughts flow from the constructions of the concept." These discursive thoughts, which are the deeds of an incorrect mental activity, flow from the conceptual constructions of the realistic belief:

> But the constructions of the concept
> Cease owing to vacuity.[14]

In other words, these realistic constructions end with the direct knowledge of emptiness.

In the original Sanskrit, this last *pada* (pair of lines) presents a form[15] that can be understood in two ways: "*owing to* emptiness" and "*in* emptiness." Under the action of the direct knowledge of emptiness, which is the antidote to the constructions of realism, the constructions of realism will cease *owing to* emptiness. Where, in what, will impurities be purified under the action of the direct knowledge of emptiness? They will be purified *in* the absolute dimension of emptiness. Hence the other reading: "*in* emptiness."

THE TRUTH OF THE WAY AND THE THREE GEMS

When the natural clear light of the mind is accompanied by substantialist discursive thoughts, the original clear light forms the terrain on which samsara turns out of these momentary realistic thoughts, which perceive emptiness in a distorted way. When the mind that has recognized its real mode, emptiness, is actually habituated to this truth, the realism[16] whose perception of the real mode of the mind is distorted is found purified in the absolute dimension of the mind itself.

As a consequence, what leads from the freedom acquired with the help of antidotes appropriate to the different negative emotions to the freedom of the essential body of buddhahood, just as what proceeds from the unimpeded path of the way of vision, the direct antidote of the negative emotions, to the absolute body of wisdom and buddhahood—all of this constitutes the noble truth of the way.[17]

The freedoms that proceed from the freedom of having eliminated certain negative emotions to the essential body of buddhahood, which is itself the freedom of having eliminated absolutely all of the negative emotions—all these freedoms constitute the truth of cessation. What leads directly to this is the truth of the way. Thus conceived, the truths of the way and of cessation represent the veritable Gem of the Dharma.

"Community of apprentices" is the name for the men and women who bear within them the qualities of cessation but have still to practice them.

"Community of those who are no longer apprentices," in other words, the buddhas, denotes the men and women who have attained the ultimate qualities, who no longer have any way to follow, who have eliminated all that was to be eliminated and possess the sum total of the qualities.

Here we have what are called the Three Gems: the Buddha, the Dharma, and the Community.

How does one take refuge in the Buddha, the Dharma, and the Community? By knowing all the details of the triple refuge, but this kind of erudition is not indispensable. The Buddha, the Dharma, and the Community are no less sublime when those who seek to take refuge in them avail themselves of the opportunity to do so in any of countless ways.

Questions and Answers III

■ ■ ■ ■

Certain people claim that it is not necessary to believe in reincarnation in order to be a Buddhist. What do you think, Your Holiness?

What is the difference between a Buddhist and a non-Buddhist? One has taken refuge [in the Three Gems], the other has not. There are, as we have seen, many ways of taking refuge. Let us envisage a person whose faith in the Three Gems is certain—myself, for example. What is my experience on this subject? I have believed in the Buddha from my early childhood. But, as I have explained, I have reflected on the way as a whole, and it is in the measure of my conviction that this reflection has permitted me to attain the boon that my faith in the Buddha has become constantly deeper.

As long as one does not have, intellectually, a clear notion of emptiness, liberation remains only a word. Then it is difficult to form the slightest correct idea of liberation, and very difficult to represent to oneself what is meant by the Awakening. It is really necessary, then, that one interested in the Awakening, who takes refuge in the state of Awakening, have a good intellectual understanding of emptiness.

And so it is that, if one begins with the Prasangika view, none of the lower Buddhist schools of thought, not even that of the Madhyamikas–Svatantrikas, has really understood the view that it is possible to have of emptiness. The Vaibhashikas, for example, treat the Madhyamika view as nihilistic: not only do they reject it but they find absolutely nothing positive there.

Nonetheless, the main reason why Buddhists see in the Buddha a thinker without peer is precisely his philosophy of the empty as interdependent production.[1] One is not a Buddhist if one believes in the Buddha while disdaining the empty and the interdependencies. I cannot render any decision, but I think, as far as I am able, that unless one admits the succession of lives it is difficult to reach omniscience, or even to conceive a clear idea of what *omniscience* means. Certain people, however, who do not believe in successive lives take refuge in the Buddha. For them, the Buddha was a great teacher of nonviolence and a great teacher, a superteacher, of compassion. What we have here is not far from Buddhist thought, but it is not enough to make one a Buddhist. I would even say that not being able to conceive an idea of reincarnation is like, for example, not being able to conceive the idea that everything is empty and interdependent.[2]

Can one deliver oneself from attachment solely by analytical meditation? Is this not a cause of frustration?

In order to gain a certitude, it is first necessary to analyze its reasons. Hence the need for analytical meditation. But at the end of this analytical meditation, when a change has taken place in the mind, whatever the object analyzed—when, therefore, the analytical mind has acquired a certain strength—it will be necessary to cling to the acquired certitude and to "unbend" completely in order to proceed to a contemplative meditation.

Chandrakirti declares that nothing has real existence, since nothing springs from itself, or from another cause, or from itself and another cause at once, or from any cause. If this is indeed the case, the causes do not really exist either. Then how does the chain of causes and effects function?

When one says that something does not exist on the level of absolute truth, what one understands by "absolute truth" consists of two things: an absolute truth for reason, which analyzes the ultimate state of an object, and an absolute truth vis-à-vis what must be refuted, that is, the real existence of an object. In the absolute truth of analytical reason, if relative phenomena exist, then their existence is absolute.

With regard to the two absolutes: Relative phenomena do not really exist on the level of the first, and their existence has nothing of the absolute on the level of the second. However, absolute truth, emptiness, is not something that really exists—by the real existence that is refuted and whose absence is an aspect of absolute truth. As emptiness has no real existence, neither does it exist on the level of the second type of absolute truth. By contrast, envisaged as that which is discovered by reason in analyzing the ultimate state of an object, emptiness really exists on the level of the first absolute truth.[3]

When it is said that something "does not exist by nature" or "by essence," one must envisage two natures or essences: a nature of things not analyzed and a nature of things that is not limited to their appearance. Up until now, we have dealt only with the essence of things as they appear. Flowers, for example, or the self, the individual: the individual is spoken of on the level of appearance alone.[4] The Buddha as well. And the Dharma. One speaks of production and cessation, which only appear. But one may wonder, when one is unsatisfied by appearances alone, whether an independent "I" exists objectively. Well, no. Then does an independent buddha exist? Again, no. An independent production? Again, no. In view of this, Nagarjuna explained in his *Fundamental Treatise* that, because they do not exist by essence, things are but "dependent designations."

What is meant by "something that does not exist by essence"? Nagarjuna answers: "Something that you do not find when you seek it." Not that what you do not find when you seek it does not exist *at all*. It exists. How? As a dependent designation.

When Nagarjuna says that things do not exist by essence because they are dependent designations, he means that what exists always exists in dependence on another thing, and thus does not exist by essence (or in itself). It is not a matter of nothingness. Were that the case, there would be nothing to find when seeking, and the sages would speak of "nothing." It is very important, then, carefully to observe the difference between "existing" and "really existing," and between "not existing at all" and "not really existing."

These flowers, for example, exist, but not really. This is why the Substantialists criticize the Madhyamikas by calling them nihilists. Asanga himself, in his *Collection of Objective Bases*[5] and his *Ten Lands*,[6] treats the Madhyamika view as nihilistic. When we can represent emptiness to ourselves as interdependent production, we no longer risk falling into nihilism. We are delivered from that. One becomes nihilistic when, on the contrary, one takes the empty for a machine for emptying everything. It is because it is empty, then, that this thing exists, and because it exists that it is empty.[7] Is it not written in the *Quintessence of Transcendent Knowledge*[8] that "form[9] is empty. Emptiness is form"?

In the first days of humanity, there were perhaps only a few hundred human beings on the earth, and they have multiplied to the point of being more than 6 billion today. How is that possible in terms of reincarnation?

How can the number of animate beings increase? If certain beings are no longer reincarnated because they have realized nirvana, population should decrease. Then where do all these beings come from?

The universe is unlimited. There are beings that come from other worlds. There are some who leave our universe to enter another universe. It seems that the galaxies are infinite. Have I ever said that the individual entity really exists? As animate beings are infinite, it is impossible to count them all: their number, then, neither increases nor decreases. Does each new creature not result from momentary causes and conditions? One should not believe that there is no beginning.

What can be done to forgive and forget past experiences that have created suffering?

We must forgive, but we must not forget. For a Buddhist, it is useful to think that one has exhausted an individual karma.[10] In evoking all of the sufferings that one has already been through, one can only rejoice at having exhausted so much karma. It would seem that the practice of exchange[11] and the fact of accepting all possible sufferings[12] secure great strength of soul and many joys. But in the particular case of those who are not interested in the Dharma, because one misfortune can always generate another, one must try to see things from several angles.

Can the karma of a father or mother influence the child? Can it be transmitted to him or her? Is there a possible relationship here?

We cannot influence karma. However, when we influence other people, we weaken their old karma by increasing their recent karma. I do not know whether karma itself is influenced.

In a world awash in armaments, murders, and injustices, what is the way that removes the negative emotions and transmutes anger into brightness of spirit and mind?

Have you had the opportunity to read the chapter devoted to "Guard of Watchfulness"[13] in *Journey Toward the Awakening?* There Shantideva says, in substance, that, the earth being covered with thorns that wound the feet, one would never have enough leather to encompass the earth, so it is better, all things considered, to cement two soles of leather onto the feet, in order to have the impression that the whole earth is covered with leather.

Vexing persons? With them the skies are replete;
Despair to span them all.
Vanquish your anger,
And you shall surely vanquish every enemy.[14]

The Bodies of the Buddha, Training, and Spiritual Masters
■ ■ ■ ■

Up to this point, I have presented to you the Three Refuges from a point of departure in the Four Noble Truths and the two fundamental truths. All religions offer a "refuge," but the Three Refuges of Buddhism present themselves as follows. Once the truth of the way has produced in the individual the Gem of the Dharma, he or she becomes a member of the sublime Community. Next, the person's psychic continuum being continuously perfected, he or she becomes a member of the Community where one is no longer an apprentice, that of the sublime buddhas. The Dharma and the Community come first, then. Only on the basis of the realization of these two levels is the level of buddha actualized.

THE FOUR BODIES OF THE BUDDHA

At this point, let us study the emergence of a teaching. First, a Buddha appeared. This Buddha pronounced the teachings of transmission. In the very act of pronouncing them, he produced in the psychic continuum of his disciples the Gem of the Dharma, which can be reduced to the truths of cessation and of the way. His disciples then constituted the Gem of the Community. The Buddha has not been the Buddha from the beginning, then. First he had to traverse the way of the apprentices. Next, he was exclusively the Buddha.

Who is Shakyamuni, the "historical" Buddha, who came up for discussion yesterday?

According to *Continuity Unexcelled*, a treatise of the Greater Vehicle, the absolute body of the Buddha, which is maintained in a state of "thusness" without ever deviating from it—that immaculate dimension that never forsakes the real, and in which all conceptual constructions are altogether stilled—has received the name "absolute body for his proper good."

What is the necessary cause of the realization of the absolute body for his proper good? One realizes the absolute body when one attaches oneself to the good of others. From that point onward, since this realization is rendered necessary by the accomplishment of the good of others, the configurations of the formal body suitable for the conversion of each person emerge spontaneously and effortlessly from the dimension of the absolute body. We are dealing with the "formal body for the good of others."

This body has two aspects. On the one hand, there is the "body of enjoyment," which constantly exists, provided with the five certitudes.[1] Generally speaking, only the sublime bodhisattvas can perceive this body—ordinary persons normally cannot. Here, then, is what is called the "body in which all enjoyments are perfect." On the other hand, we have the "body of apparition," so named because it appears, or manifests itself, in fields that have not been purified by the body of enjoyment, to ordinary persons whose karma is sufficiently pure.

And so it is that the thousand and one Buddhas who honor this Good Era[2] with their presence, and they alone, are supreme bodies of apparition. Conqueror Shakyamuni is the fourth of these guides. Protector Maitreya, the future Buddha, will be the fifth. Some claim that Maitreya is already here. I do not believe so. The texts only mean that, long after the disappearance of the teachings of the Buddha, Lion of the Shakyas, the protector Maitreya will come—not that he has already left his place of concealment and is gradually approaching.

Now for the four bodies. What are they?

The absolute body is divided into the absolute body of wisdom and the essential body.

The absolute body of wisdom is nothing but the wisdom that directly knows all of the phenomena designated by the two fundamental truths. How can this be? When one possesses the qualities of enfranchisement and release, which result from the elimination of the cognitive veil impeding the simultaneous perception of the two truths, it becomes possible to realize omniscient wisdom. That is why the Buddha's absolute body of wisdom is distinguished from his essential body.

The essential body, in turn, has two aspects: the essential body suddenly pure, and the essential body naturally pure.

The essential body suddenly pure is spoken of in reference to the release of one who has eliminated all impurities. And this ability is an effect of this person's natural purity itself. The essential body of the Buddha, then, has two aspects; reduced to a single body, they constitute the essential body. The four bodies, then, are the essential body, the absolute body, the body of enjoyment, and the body of apparition. In the Unsurpassable Tantras, we find minuscule differences in the definition of the four bodies.

Nonetheless, the Vaibhashikas maintain that the Buddha first realized nirvana without residues, and that, subsequently, the stream of his consciousness was interrupted. His continuum ceased, like the flame of an extinguished lamp. In the system of the four bodies, we hear it explained that the configurations of the body of apparition are deployed from a point of departure in the body of enjoyment, and that the body of enjoyment transmits the configurations of the body of apparition and reabsorbs them.

The Buddha did not publicly teach the sutras of the Greater Vehicle. They are teachings intended for certain individuals with a purified karma, more particularly in relation to the teachings proper to the adamantine Vehicle of the Secret Formulas, which addresses a still more restricted number of individuals.

When the Buddha taught the configurations of the body of enjoyment and the body of apparition, then, he did so not under his aspect of historical Buddha but subsequently under other aspects.

It is impossible to say whether, for example, the mystical cycles emanating from visions seen by the masters of our generation are all worthy of faith. In order for such a cycle to be authentic and worthy of confidence, it must emanate from a perfectly clear vision of a particular deity of the Three Roots,[3] as clearly as when two people meet. And in this way beings like Shakyamuni or Nagarjuna can still appear today, to those whose karma is pure. This is not the effect of interior discourse, nor the fruit of the imagination. It is really as when two people meet and the one receives teachings from the other, or poses questions to resolve his or her doubts.

Takloung Shapdroung Rinpoche[4] has told me an interesting story on this subject. One day, when Dilgo Khyentsé Rinpoche[5] was receiving from him certain Taklounga teachings in Nepal, at the precise moment that he was transmitting to him a certain section of a particular cycle, Khyentsé Rimpoche saw clearly, on the surface of the beams of the ceiling, his principal masters and the masters of the lineage of this cycle, all of them teaching. Takloung Shabdroung is a true, good, aged lama. He has spent many years in Chinese prisons. He entertains not the least hope or the least apprehension, and never would he profit from a lie.

Consequently, the experience that each person, according to his or her capacities, has or has had, must have the force of an astonishing experience like that one. If one admits the system of the four bodies, these are things that one can explain. But if one does not admit the system of the four bodies, it is impossible.

TRAINING IN THE WAY

In what respect are the Three Gems refuges, and how can we "take refuge" in them? We can take refuge in the Buddha, the Dharma, and the Community, which we have just seen, placing our hope in them. One who does this becomes a member of the Community, and this should produce in his or her psychic continuum the Jewel of the Dharma, which consists in cessation and a way.

One can also take refuge by swearing to do everything necessary for awakening in a manifest, perfect fashion. Of these two takings of refuge, the second is the more important. But is it possible, when one has sworn to reach buddhahood, to realize the level of the Three Gems—to actualize, oneself, ultimate buddhahood? This is what is answered by the "potential," or "nature," of buddha.

The Chittamatrins, too, for example, postulate that there are ultimately three vehicles. If, for example, I have realized the awakening of the Hearers, I cannot go further. And it is impossible for an eremitic buddha to be enlightened more than in the awakening of the eremitic buddhas. On the hypothesis that certain families of beings can reach buddhahood (and certain others not),[6] there are Buddhists who judge this distinction ultimately true, then, in three vehicles of realization.

Still, in the Middle Way, if we admit the temporary existence of precise, determinate families, we recognize that ultimately those who belong to the three families[7] are all of the people capable of reaching perfect buddhahood. The adepts of the Middle Way, then, agree that ultimately there is but a single vehicle.[8]

If this is the way things are, then how should one train? Of the four truths, the one called the truth of the way is the principal way, the sublime way. To engender qualities like those of the sublime way, one must at this point train along a way that commences on the level of the beginners.

In brief, the qualities of the sublime way are twofold: the qualities tied up with abandonment of, or enfranchisement and release from, the negative emotions, and the qualities of realization. While we cannot immediately eliminate what has to be eliminated, we have to begin abstaining from it at once. We simply cannot enjoy qualities of realization of the sublime wisdom instantly, but we ought to be able to cultivate certain qualities that tend toward this realization.

Now all of this can be reduced to the triple training: discipline, recollection, and knowledge.

In his *Four Hundred Stanzas*,[9] Aryadeva writes:

First, to arrest the nonmeritorious.
Next, to refute the self.
Last, to dissipate all opinions:
Master this, and you are a sage.

In other words, we must first of all abstain from nonmeritorious acts—those that project into bad destinies.[10] Second, we must do away with belief in the "I." And third, we must utterly reject our entire deplorable tendency to nurse opinions.

In his *Lamp of the Way*,[11] Atisha Dipamkara speaks of small, medium, and great beings. There are various ways of explaining what Aryadeva means by "refute the self" and "dissipate all opinions," but I think that we can envisage these ideas in terms of these three types of beings.

In order to train along the way, one must first acquire what is called knowledge born of hearing [or of study]. Next, one must reflect on what one has learned from others, each one alone, by ceaselessly repeating the exercise that combines analysis and contemplation, until one has certitude of having found what one sought. This is the second knowledge, knowledge born of reflection. When, subsequently, we meditate by concentrating [on this "indubitable discovery"], and reach an authentic experience, we experience what is called knowledge born of meditation.

When we seek an inner conviction, we begin by letting go of the prejudices that spring from the distorted perception of things, and we are forced to doubt. Then, in thrusting the reflection forward, we arrive at a strictly intellectual understanding: we tell ourselves that perhaps we have found what we sought. In pursuing this trajectory, in reasoning without respite, we reach a decisive conclusion, a deep certitude: now it is a matter of a true knowledge emerging from deductive reasoning. Finally, when we have acquired a solid habit of this truth, and have a clear vision of the object of our meditation, we have what is called effective habituation.

To eliminate the mistaken concepts that result from fixation on an extreme, it is important to have recourse to the *prasanga*, and in order to draw a correct deduction, to logical reasoning. When, in common language, we say, "This thing does not exist," that resembles *prasanga,* and when we say, "This is that," this is somewhat as if we were reasoning. On the *prasanga* and reasoning, the masters Dingnaga and Dharmakirti have written a great deal. These are essential subjects. The *prasanga* and reasoning are, however, meant not for debate with others but for "discussion" in one's own thought, between the mistaken concept and the correct thought, somewhat like the debate in *Journey Toward the Awakening* in the chapter entitled "Meditative Concentration," between love of self and love of others.

And so, when one practices individually, one must debate. When one practices, one reflects, and the mistaken thought of the adversary advances reasons to the contrary. It will explain that it is like this, that this is what it believes, and one must contradict it. It is in this sense that hearing, which represents the first step in knowledge of the teachings, must obey an essential rule: to avoid all possible deviations in the manner of following the master who instructs us.

The explanatory instructions consist mainly of various approaches to eliminate false conceptions. When the emphasis is placed no longer there but on practice itself, the instructions follow the experiences of the one meditating, and we speak of instructions for practice.

It can also be that the master begins with the few succinct instructions necessary to a meditation session and has the pupil meditate. This can last one or two years. When, in meditating, the disciple attains realization, the master gives him or her the instructions of the following phase. As long as the pupil does not have experience, he or she will not receive other instructions. When the pupil has had an experience, the instructions received are called instructions on experience.

One cannot scatter the darkness of ignorance until one has lighted the torch of hearing. Indeed, unless one has eliminated false conceptions by hearing, meditation will be confused at best. If one has not formed the least conviction, one will wonder whether this is not right, unless it be this other, and so on. In a word, one runs the great risk of imitating those who always believe the last one to speak. Nonetheless, when we study without controlling our mind, we feed our pride with the Dharma and criticize everything. When this happens, it is as if the medicine had turned to poison.

Those who proclaim that the essential thing is practice, and that there is no need to hear teachings—those who stubbornly hold to practicing, declaring that study is not necessary—cannot eliminate their false conceptions and, in the guise of meditation, only narrate to themselves that they have found the Three Gems. When you really think about it, these people are sure of nothing.

In this sense, the scholar is not worth more than the upright person, nor the upright person more than the scholar. Scholarship and inner accomplishment are both necessary. But without the qualities of goodness as the crown of the whole, one will think only of one's own personal good, and that is useless.

It is generally useful to gain instruction by reading. But it is essential that someone present us, in terms of experience, with what the books teach. This is where the spiritual master becomes primary. The Buddha taught what are called the four charms. He taught them mainly for the accomplishment of the good of others, while the six transcendent virtues are intended for the good of the one practicing them. The four charms are material generosity, agreeable discourse, obligingness, and adaptation.[12]

Obligingness and adaptation mean, respectively, that the master will attract the disciple by being likable, and that each disciple will practice the teachings that are suitable for him or her personally. Here again is an essential point.

THE SPIRITUAL MASTER

To return to the four bodies of the Buddha, accomplished buddhahood, for example, has been manifested under the aspect of a supreme body of apparition. For six years the Buddha gave himself over to the mortifications of asceticism for our good. For that matter, I say as an aside that we are wrong if we believe that we can practice the Dharma without tiring ourselves and leave mortifications to the Buddha. The other day I was joking with a Christian monk. I told him, "Jesus went to a lot of trouble. If people believe that it is enough to do this [His Holiness makes the sign of the cross] in a church, they are mistaken."

The master is the one who shows. He himself gives us the example of what is to be done. And so, Jesus, Muhammad, and all of the great masters show their disciples the way. In this we see the importance of the spiritual master.

If we wish to follow a spiritual master, then, it is very important to see first whether he combines all the characteristics of an authentic master. If a preacher announces that he is about to teach the Dharma, we may go and hear him, but we need not immediately consider him our master.

Take this meeting of ours, for example. Is this a lecture or a teaching? We have to see. We absolutely have to observe, over the course of several years, whether the one who is speaking acts in conformity with what he or she says. I constantly tell journalists to have a long nose, to examine things. We continuously hear of the "private life." Is there a life that could be private? There would not have to be. Really, one need only be as open in private as in public. To show something in public and act otherwise in private is not the way to proceed. It is a lie. It is indispensable, then, to examine one's master well. Otherwise we run the risk of falling into a kind of cult of personality. And Buddhists are not immune to this type of danger.

Well aware of all this, the Buddha taught the characteristics of the spiritual master and recommended our careful examination of him in order to avoid any form of cult. And it is again in support of these teachings that we read in the *Rule of the Holy Dharma* that we must not heed masters who "maintain things contrary to the Dharma." And so, in the sutras of the Greater Vehicle, the Buddha says that the friend in good [or friend of good, the spiritual master] acts in the direction of virtue, and not the contrary. Similarly, we read in the *Fifty Stanzas on the Spiritual Master*[13] these lines, which describe the manner of following a master of the Unsurpassable Tantras:

> What does not contravene reason,
> This it is that must be practiced.

In other words, after having examined the reasons for a particular declaration by the master, if we experience the least uneasiness when comparing them with the general system taught by the Buddha, then we ought not to apply them. But we must not stop here either. The texts specify that we should then try to understand why it would not be correct to apply this indication of the master, considering the general line of the teachings.

I am sometimes concerned about students whose minds never stay still. They are too much open to influence and believe that those who are said to have many disciples are true masters. And they throw themselves at their feet. This is not the thing to do. Be careful.

Before following a master, then, you must read many books and understand them well. Next, once you have the opportunity, examine the master, and if after this examination you think that you have really found an authentic master, then it is well to make him your spiritual master.

Unless one begins with this examination, the practice of what is called union with the natural state of the master[14] will be extremely burdensome. One should not commit oneself after merely groping about, without previous examination, and this is especially true when one is choosing a spiritual master. One must not commit oneself at random without well examining the person one intends to follow.

TRAINING FOR DISCIPLINE

When we move on to practice, the first thing we encounter is training for discipline. At this point, whether or not they have received particular vows, all Buddhists begin with a general recognition of the ten nonvirtuous acts; then they adopt as their discipline the avoidance of these acts. They first commit themselves to the practice that consists of forbidding oneself behaviors harmful to the body, the word, and the mind. In this they follow the discipline that consists of renouncing the ten nonvirtuous acts, which lays the foundations that will make it possible to reach the truth of cessation.

When the practice of renouncing the ten nonvirtuous acts has been well integrated, one must reflect on the effects of acts.[15] And in reflecting on causality, one observes that, if we register a beneficial cause, it will have happiness as its effect. If we register a harmful cause, it will have suffering as its effect. And this is the way to understand the relationship of cause and effect.

In order to know the disadvantages of the nonmeritorious, the negative act, we must know the places of birth of the evil destinies.[16] We must come to know how one lives in the lower worlds. And when we think of the sufferings of the evil destinies, we must tell ourselves not that these will be "evil" only in some remote future but rather that, because the hour of death is uncertain,[17] if one has registered causes of rebirth in the evil destinies, one may be very near them already.

It is imperative, then, that we reflect on the four subjects that turn the mind from samsara. These are the first foundations upon which we shall turn our mind toward the Dharma, and it is upon them that we shall build everything else. Otherwise the teachings will remain but lovely words.

Discouragement in the face of difficulty is a very serious defect.

Whether one is a practitioner or an ordinary person, it is an exceptionally grave shortcoming to lose courage. Hence the importance of contemplating the freedoms and the riches.[18] It is not enough to have a "buddha potential." We must have won, besides, the support of a body "free and rich." It is because we have the potential of becoming a buddha that the fact of having won this human body at this point is of such great importance: it is the opportunity to deal it a good swat. And this is what Aryadeva means by "renouncing the nonmeritorious."

What does the Dharma enable its practitioners to accomplish? Liberation. And the greatest obstacle to the accomplishment of liberation consists in the negative emotions. What is meant by *liberation*? Victory over the negative emotions. The enemy, then, is the negative emotions, the very things that, from everlasting, have tortured us. If a spiritual teaching directly or indirectly attacks the negative emotions, it is Buddhist. Otherwise it is not. If paranormal knowledge and magical powers do not attack the negative emotions, then they have nothing to do with Buddhism.

So we have a means of constantly measuring ourselves with regard to the negative emotions. Since we have once been subject to them, we must now avoid the harmful behaviors that the negative emotions have the power to provoke. Subsequently, we shall eliminate them only by applying to them their direct antidotes. Finally, we will have to destroy the habitual schemata that the negative emotions have inscribed in us.

Questions and Answers IV

■ ■ ■ ■

How can one assist a dying person? Can positive thoughts be of some help here? You said yesterday that we remain in the clear light for three days. Then what do you think of organ transplants? And what do you think of a cremation that may occur right after death?

The most important thing is for the mind to depart in peace, in all repose and calm. Whether it has religious convictions or not, the essential thing is for it to depart without care. Indeed, if it has a religious belief, we must adapt to it. It is generally impossible to return to life after the experience of the clear light. When the clear light has ceased, it is impossible to return to life. I think, then, that it is perfect to make a gift of one's organs to help others. If there is a cremation in which the body of the deceased is burned, it is better, as far as possible, to leave the body in peace for a while, until there is an odor—until the first signs of decomposition manifest themselves.

What do you think of suicide?

It is always better not to commit suicide. To take the example of the transfer of consciousness:[1] when we are afflicted with a fatal disease and there is no longer any way to prolong our life, we are compelled to proceed with that life before having lost all of our strength for it, and before the dissolution of the physical elements. The premature transfer presents the disadvantage of killing deities. The right moment to die is when we are certain that we are going to die, when it is no longer possible to live—in brief, when death is no longer doubtful and before the physical elements are not really too feeble. Here there is no suicide. The practice of the transfer is inevitably a suicide if there is still hope for life. Here it is preferable to do nothing.

Yesterday you spoke a great deal of antidotes. Can you give some examples?

The antidote to hatred is meditation on love, and the one for craving and attachment is meditation on the unclean, or foul. The antidote for pride consists in studying the phenomena whose categories are innumerable, poring over subjects like the aggregates, the elements, the sensory organs, because in this fashion we finally recognize that we know nothing, and we lose a bit of our conceit. Myself, for example—I always think I'm intelligent, and I become a bit prideful. When that happens to me, I imagine myself sitting at a computer, and I tell myself that I don't understand anything, that I'm not very sharp.

The antidote for ignorance is, especially, wisdom. All the other antidotes act indirectly on the negative emotions, and can only reduce their intensity without destroying them completely. The absolute antidote that can destroy them completely, their "direct antidote," the one that can eliminate everything fit for elimination, is direct knowledge of emptiness. But this consciousness that knows emptiness directly cannot act fully from the moment of its discovery. It must be continuously intensified, and when the wisdom arises that realizes emptiness in the union of quietude and the higher vision, then it will act as the direct antidote of everything fit for elimination.

Can animals attain the Awakening?

They will be able to. As we have seen, it is said that all animate beings have the power to become a buddha. But animals are, as it were, deprived of this, for one must practice in order for this potential to be realized. And without human discernment, it is difficult to practice.

Yesterday you mentioned how ignorance, subtle attachment, proceeded from the clear light of the mind. Why and how does this subtle attachment come in the first place?

It is in the nature of things. It is not that the natural wisdom that existed before gradually encountered ignorance. Ignorance exists from time without a beginning. In certain texts, for example, it is said that our pure awakening, Samantabhadra,[2] the primordial protector, existed before the separation of samsara and nirvana. Here there must be consideration of the state of an individual who has just died, and whose dimension of innate original light is not veiled by any sullying from outside. I cannot conceive that there was Samantabhadra, the primordial protector, before, then the separation of samsara and nirvana, and that subsequently samsara and nirvana gradually separated.

You have spoken of the continuum of the clear light of consciousness without beginning, without end, and without external causes or conditions. Does this not come down to what other traditions call God or self?

In a sense, the clear light is a creator, but only in a sense. Buddhism accepts self-creation,[3] or "production from a point of departure in oneself." So we must envision this mode of creation with respect to the clear light. However, *my* clear light has uniquely created *my* lives, and never the lives of others. My clear light participates only in the formation of the world that is common to us. If your aggregates exist, this is hardly because my own clear light has created them.

As for the *atman*, the self, it designates a unique, eternal entity. Now, because the clear light forms an uninterrupted continuum, it has the permanence of continuity and the impermanence of the instants that compose it. I am not saying that the clear light is the individual. The innate original clear light is not the self. It is not the referent of the designation "self"; it is not the *atman*. To speak as does the *Guhyasamaja*, there exist a very subtle consciousness and a very subtle body.

Just as on the basis of the gross body and consciousness we speak of the gross individual, on the basis of the very subtle body and consciousness we speak of the very subtle individual.

Without concepts, would truth be relative?

For the Chittamatrins, form and all external phenomena represent but the apparent aspect of the mind, in the interior. Their essence is that of mind. They are not two different things. In stating this, one is not far from saying that, regardless of the phenomenon envisaged, it exists while the consciousness of the one apprehending it lasts. And when this consciousness is extinguished, the phenomenon no longer exists.

This holds for the consciousness that, in my continuum, apprehends the flowers and for the flowers themselves. But this does not mean that, when I have left, these flowers will cease to exist.

Likewise, are these flowers that I see the same as the ones that you see? No satisfactory answer is possible. Have they the same nature as my consciousness, as your consciousness? It is difficult to say. It is a real problem. For the Chittamatrins, who explain that an object is "certain" once it is simultaneous with the consciousness that perceives it,[4] the flowers exist when consciousness of the flowers exists and they cease when this consciousness ceases. But it is hard for me to explain their view.

To answer the question, it is indeed not a matter of resorbing our conceptual conceptions. Let us return to the example of that visual consciousness that apprehends forms. If I think of impermanence, for example, or of the spirit of Awakening, which is love and compassion, when I look at the flowers, I have "drawn my mind back" from its construction "flowers." Which does not mean, however, that the flowers themselves no longer exist. If they had to disappear because we find ourselves in a nondiscursive state of wisdom, or again from the angle of the absolute dimension in which constructions of the concept are entirely quenched, then from the very fact that the mind of the buddhas and bodhisattvas is only nondiscursive wisdom, these persons would have absolutely no more conceptual constructions. But when we hear of the "quenching of all discursive thoughts," what is being described is the functioning of individual thought, not the disappearance of objects.

How may we increase our attention in everyday life?

This comes down to habituating oneself to attention. The Thai adepts of vipassana meditation are particularly strong when it comes to the reinforcement of attention. When they take a step, they think, "Now I am lifting my right foot." With the following step, "Now I am lifting my left foot." Every moment, they keep their attention taut and thus acquire the habit of always paying attention. Those, that is, who are perfect.

Otherwise, it can be useful to write "Attention, Attention!" pretty much everywhere in the house you live in. It should be written even in the toilets and on the hands. That way, once you see the word *attention,* you have the opportunity to make progress. The adepts of the yogas of the dream know this kind of practice. On everything that they might see throughout the day, they write the word *dream,* and when they are permeated with its meaning, it is easy for them to recognize that everything is as a dream.

You have said that every continuum of luminous mind is individual, and that this continuum remains individual when an individual becomes a buddha. How can that be reconciled with the fact that the buddhas all have the same nature, in other words that essentially they are one?

We have the same nature, you and I. Essentially, you are buddhas, and I am as well. You are human beings, and I am as well. We are similar. We have not had to fuse for that. The "essence" of the buddhas is one, because it designates their equality in terms of release and realization. The "equal savor" bears on the equality of at least two entities. We cannot speak of equality apropos of one thing. Were we but one, we could not "have the same savor."

It is said that everything has the same savor in the dimension of the real. In the space of emptiness, we all have the same savor. This is also valid for samsara and nirvana, or good and evil. Constructions of the concept all have the same savor in the free space of constructions. This does not, however, mean that constructions of the concept are not different from one another.

Have men and women the same power to become a buddha?

Of course. We read in the *Treasury of Scholasticism* that, for the Vaibhashikas, the one who registers the karma that will ripen into "major notes"[5] begins by accumulating merits over the course of three great kalpas beyond measure, and finally must still register, throughout one hundred kalpas, the particular karma that will ripen into major and minor notes of the Buddha. Throughout these one hundred last kalpas, the practitioner will have a male body. This is how the *Treasury* sees things. In the sutra system as well, one must have the body of a man in order to reach the Great Awakening.

In the Unsurpassable Tantras, there are women who become buddhas in this support, the body of a woman. The awesome Tara,[6] for example, became a buddha as a woman. When she engendered the spirit of Awakening[7] for the first time, it was as a woman. There are many men who have become buddhas, not many women. So Tara said, As long as I shall work at accumulations (of merits and wisdom), and until I awaken in manifest and perfect manner, I shall no longer be reborn except as a woman. I shall awaken to buddhahood as a woman—in the body of a woman.

Tara was the most vigorous of feminists.

Refutation of the Self

■ ■ ■ ■

We have finished, then, with Aryadeva's first phase: "to arrest the nonmeritorious." "Next, to refute the self" means to meditate on gross insubstantiality, or the "unreality of the individual self." Although it does not have the strength to uproot the negative emotions, this meditation has the strength to weaken them. "Last, to dissipate all opinions" is the third and final phase.

During the second phase, refuting the self, one is familiarized with all the characteristics of individual insubstantiality. But it is in directly knowing the subtle insubstantiality of the individual that one truly eliminates the negative emotions. These phases both lead to liberation.

In the ancient Indian religious tradition, some people believed in the succession of lives and others did not. Among those who did, some believed in liberation, and others did not. And among those who believed in liberation, some saw it as a pure field—a paradise. We can read in the sacred texts of the Naked Ascetics,[1] for example, that "liberation" is a place like a reversed white parasol.

For Buddhists, liberation concerns spiritual qualities. In a word, as long as one remains in the grip of the negative emotions, one will not know a moment of happiness. It is liberation from emotional ties, then, that is called liberation.

THE PRACTICE OF MENTAL QUIETUDE

In order to repel the negative emotions, there is quietude,[2] which opposes the manifest, or gross emotions, sometimes impossible to conquer otherwise. To eradicate the emotions and their seeds, there is knowledge. Among the three types of knowledge, as we have seen in relation to the direct antidote to the negative emotions, we are concerned here with direct knowledge of emptiness.

There is a whole spectrum of knowledge: direct knowledge of impermanence, direct knowledge of the void of autonomous and substantial individual existence, and a good many others. As for the direct antidote to all the negative emotions, it is direct knowledge or cognition of subtle emptiness, of subtle insubstantiality—the emptiness of which we have already spoken a bit.

In order for meditative recollection to integrate quietude and the higher vision,[3] the factors of quietude must be cultivated. An increase in the power of attention[4] and watchfulness permits the attainment of quietude of mind. One may use one's attention and watchfulness as one pleases, the goal being to attain a state of quiet concentration.

The practice of attention and watchfulness begins with training for discipline, which is threefold: individual liberation, the spirit of Awakening, and the tantras. Individual liberation is addressed to devout laypersons and to religious. In the discipline of the devout laity, there are rules to be followed all one's life, and rules to be followed for a certain number of days or number of times.

In order to put one or another of these rules into practice, we ask ourselves whether we are not going to contravene it by acting in a particular way. We concentrate on the question, then, and if we realize that we are on the verge of acting badly, in action or in word, we recall that it is unsuitable for us to slip. When we remember that a particular bad action is not permitted, we have recourse to the guardian of watchfulness, to ask ourselves whether we have not united all the elements constituting a bad action. We then recall that this action is unworthy, and we see in it a true danger. Watchfulness uncovers this risk and permits us to avoid it. So it is that, with the aid of attention, watchfulness, and interest, we seek to respect discipline.

The discipline of individual liberation[5] consists essentially in avoiding bad actions of body and word. Its principal aim is the individual Awakening. The discipline of the bodhisattvas emphasizes the control of misdeeds of the mind: one simply prohibits oneself from accepting that one's own interest comes before that of others. As for the tantric vows, I cannot summarize them as I have the other two. Know that they are truly many.

How can one reach a recollection of attention and watchfulness? Here, mental quietude constitutes an essential practice, one at the heart of the Buddhist teachings. Before the Buddha taught, the practice of recollection already existed, just as did a higher vision of the world that presented subtle and gross aspects. In those days, however, the higher vision that consists in knowing directly, and correctly, the insubstantiality of all phenomena was practically unknown. But we can say that Buddhism borrowed practices common to pre-Buddhist Indian literature. It could even be that the Dharma borrows certain practices from the traditions of these, our mystical friends. And Christians, for example, and others may borrow certain things from the Dharma.

By nature, quietude is neutral. Motivated by renunciation, it is a cause of liberation. Motivated by the spirit of Awakening, it is a cause of omniscience. And attached to the view of the self, it is a non-Buddhist quietude. Overall, quietude is especially a contemplative meditation, and the higher vision [or "penetrating"], an analytical meditation. One must first accomplish quietude, we hear it explained, and only afterwards practice the higher vision. Still, the Unsurpassable Tantras proclaim the practice of contemplative meditation right in the higher vision, which is direct knowledge of emptiness. The Unsurpassable Tantras, then, urge a meditation in a unity of quietude and the higher vision.

In order to attain quietude, we must first understand the meaning of the word *quietude*—in Tibetan, *shi-nè:* literally, "peaceful state." *Peaceful* denotes the perfect "pacification" or extinction of distraction—mental projections stirred by thoughts other than the object of concentration—and this pacification permits the practitioner to remain in a state of balanced mind, in all concentration. We can now speak of quiet concentration. When we pursue our meditation in continuity with what the word *quietude* precisely denotes—a perfect recollection of concentration—gradually the body and mind feel the pleasure of a peaceful buoyancy.[6] One reaches concentration of mind on these conditions alone.

There are three worlds and nine levels,[7] among which the four *dhyanas,* or concentrations, occupy levels two through five.

The first concentration is composed of concentration properly so called and two preparatory recollections. So when we reach the recollection of concentration called "preparation in which there is nothing that cannot be"[8] we reach, to put it briefly, the first qualities of the recollection of the higher worlds.[9] Here we have what is called quietude. It is only when one reaches the preparatory concentration of the first dhyana, then, that analytical meditation begins.

In analytical meditation, we direct our attention to a correct understanding of the character of the higher and lower spheres of existence. We then proceed to the five other exercises of attention.[10] Next we come to the resulting "four spheres of infinite perception,"[11] beginning with the first concentration properly so called, which is followed by the second, third, and fourth concentrations: namely, the spheres of perception of the unlimited space of the world Without Form, of unlimited consciousness, and of nothingness and the neither-being-nor-not-being, all the way to the summit of becoming.[12] So recollection becomes more and more profound, and more and more subtle.

At this point let us see the objects of concentration of quietude. In order to resolve doubts on this subject, it is explained that there is a universal object, objects that purify acts (objects of erudition[13]), and objects that purify the negative emotions.

The object of general and universal concentration[14] belongs both to quietude and to the higher vision. Thus, for those who, in the course of their previous lives, or even in the first part of their present lives, have acted under the influence of powerful negative emotions, there are various objects of concentration corresponding to various individual constitutions and called "objects that purify acts." These objects are adapted to the strength of the individual's propensities to attachment and hatred. "Objects that purify the negative emotions" are various concentrations directly corresponding to specific emotions.

We can, broadly speaking, take as our support of concentration a representation of the Buddha. For Christians, this can be a representation of Jesus or of the Virgin Mary. One may even concentrate on flowers. But if we take as our support of concentration something like a flower, we must not concentrate on an external flower. We must concentrate on the image of the flower that appears to the mind—on a "reflection for recollection" or mental object represented by the image of a flower. There we have the object of concentration of recollection. In the beginning, to form a habit and not allow ourselves to be distracted by the senses, it will be necessary to take as our object of concentration the mental image of a being like the Buddha.

SPECIFIC INSTRUCTIONS ON MEDITATION

When one meditates, the position of the body is essential. One crosses one's legs in a lotus, or half lotus, position.[15] Those among you who are not accustomed to sitting tailor fashion, or who have bad knees, do not be concerned. All that counts is to be comfortably seated. Next, one straightens one's backbone like an arrow; the shoulders fall naturally; and one bends one's neck very slightly. This way, if we fall asleep, we shall snore less loudly—make less noise.

When one has bent the neck slightly, one places one's hands four finger widths below the navel, the right over the left, flat, so that the tips of the thumbs touch; the elbows are not glued to the body; the jaws and lips are in a natural position; the point of the tongue is on the roof of the mouth; and the eyes are fixed on the end of the nose.

The Dzogchen[16] speak of "three immobilities," of which the first qualifies the regard that contemplates space. But for the moment it is the end of one's nose that one must look at. You who have pointed noses, you can do this with no trouble. You who have flat noses, if you look at the tip of your nose, pretty soon your eyes start to hurt. Do you find this hard to do? Do you understand? We are told that, generally speaking, when one is very erect, the end of the nose is straight above the navel. In other words, a pebble that falls from the tip of the nose will fall square on the navel. If you have a big stomach, you are a special case. For that matter, my stomach, too, is getting larger.

On inhaling and exhaling, there are also some essential points. One must breathe softly, without forcing it, and not in an irregular rhythm. What they call "chasing the corpses away with nine breaths"[17] is a way of getting rid of the residual air in the lungs in nine exhalations, but—should I mention this?—in the tantric practices, as in the techniques of Naropa, movements must be made that purify the body. So it is unnecessary to count.

For the moment, then, we shall close the left nostril with the right forefinger. In practice, you begin with the right or the left, this is not the place to discuss that detail. We close the left nostril with the flat of the nail of the forefinger. We slowly inhale and exhale. Likewise, we close the right nostril with the left hand. We inhale, we exhale. Then we inhale through both nostrils.

In the tantras, this breathing exercise is performed according to particular schemata, like the three channels, or the five wheels.[18] Not here. Then what are we going to do?

We must ensure that our various thoughts are "equalized." Once captive, the mind is not allowed to attend to anything but the inhalation and exhalation. While inhaling we think that we are inhaling, and while exhaling, that we are exhaling, without allowing ourselves to think of anything else, and when we no longer think of anything but the in-and-out of the breathing, if we expel the residual breath nine times, our mental excitation may diminish.

When we have adopted the physical posture I just described, if we visualize the object of concentration outside the body, it will be found at the level of the bridge of the nose, no more than two arm's lengths, or about two yards, away. We may also visualize it within our body, in the body's special places [for example, the chakras].

Whatever the object of concentration, it must not be visualized large one day and small the next. It should remain the same size. One begins, then, by representing it to oneself mentally. The mental image is maintained with the help of the attention of memory and is guarded by watchfulness, so that the mind will not be distracted from its object of concentration or allow itself to be overcome by confusion.

What are the qualities necessary for the mind that has fixed upon a recollection of concentration? It should remain on the object of concentration, but this aspect is not the only one. This mind must be an intelligence awake, clear, and transparent. That which prevents the mind from remaining fixed on its object is the work of the scattering factor.

Even if the mind stays on its object, its clear, transparent, and precise nondistraction can succumb to torpor. At times, when one has not the slightest thought on one's mind, when darkness of mind has supervened, one has the experience of torpor. Torpor is the cause of hebetude, or lethargy.

And so, both torpor and scatteredness present gross, subtle, and very subtle levels. It is easy to identify gross torpor and scatteredness. And it is easy to apply to them the appropriate antidote. The more they become subtle, the more difficult it is to recognize them and apply an antidote.

When one has too lively a mind, too alert, the risk is scatteredness. The antidote to scatteredness consists in having one's thoughts "come back down." In the case of depression, the mind is at its lowest. But when it is totally scattered, one must bring it back down, and return within. If the mind is less alert, less lively, the danger is of sinking into torpor. All of this can be read in the texts, but the absolutely essential comes from experience.

When, for example, one concentrates too strongly, one has a tendency to sink a bit. In order to bring one's mind up, one thinks of something joyous. Likewise, in practicing analysis the mind often is raised too high. It is then necessary to observe carefully what is occurring, each one in his or her own experience, and to try to keep the mind at the right level.

When you pour water on earth or sand, the water risks flowing to the left as well as to the right. Whichever direction it takes, a means must be found to stop it. In the same fashion, wherever the failing comes from—torpor or scatteredness—one must have recourse to antidotes, and not only keep the mind on its object but have it clear, vivid, and precise. This is how one must meditate.

At first, the sole concern is to "pose" the mind on the object of concentration. When one can extend somewhat the posed continuum of the mind, we hear of gently "re-posing" it. We shall continue by bringing back the mind, whose quietude most often is scattered with the speed of lightning—posing the mind, posing it lastingly, re-posing it, subduing it, laying it to rest, laying it to rest perfectly, concentrating it on a single point, and leaving it at one with itself. These are the nine "stations" of the mind.[19] Gradually the aspect of "calm" is projected on the object of concentration.

When the risks of torpor and scatteredness have diminished, when we are freed from them, effort is found to be less and less necessary, and ultimately not necessary at all. At that point we shall decide, at the beginning of the meditation session, to deliver ourselves to a faultless recollection: in the course of this session, we shall not allow ourselves to be possessed by torpor and scatteredness. With this decision made, we finally traverse the nine stations without the slightest effort, just as when we recite our habitual prayers.

Next, when we are able to spend a long time without the threats of torpor and scatteredness—perfectly concentrated on the object of meditation—then and only then, little by little, flexibility of body and mind make their appearance. Once the pleasure of these flexibilities has entered the picture, the two "gladnesses" induced by the flexibilities will gradually appear.

In any event, what is called the resistance[20] of body and mind is that which, when we employ mind and body for the good, prevents them from doing it freely; resistance is not the fact of not wishing to practice the good. On the level of intention, everyone wishes to do good, but there is something that depends on the physical and psychic dispositions that prevents the person from surrendering to the good with ease. Once one has been gradually delivered from this resistance of body and mind, therefore, one can employ the body and mind for virtuousness.

When we have come to this kind of meditative recollection, our mind is extremely clear and stable. The strength of gross attachment and hatred, as well as powerful effects of the same order, diminishes enormously. Among Tibetans who have gone to India, not many, but certain ones it would appear, know this very particular experience.

One can also choose as one's object of concentration, in view of quietude, the mind itself. The "mind" here denotes consciousness ceaselessly perpetuated. Most of the time thought is scattered to the outside, and as we are not constantly observing the essence of our mind, when it is necessary to define this mind, we are only able to repeat that the mind, or more precisely consciousness, is a simple experience of knowledge and clarity.

It is difficult to represent to ourselves, in experience itself, the clear, knowing, and "experiential" nature of the mind. We cannot form the least idea of it for ourselves. We must strive, and strive some more, to have the experience of the qualities of knowledge and clarity proper to consciousness.

The mind very closely follows external objects: forms, sounds, odors, tastes, and what can be touched. The visual consciousness, for example, is that which apprehends forms. The thought that represents the form to itself seems to have a form itself. If this is the case, the clear and knowing essence of the mind is veiled by the form. We must renounce memories, then, all of these thoughts in which we evoke a particular past experience, not permitting them to return, just as we shall not permit free flow to hopes and fears relative to the future.

Let us use the analogy of a stream. As long as a stream is flowing, we cannot see its bed. But if we stop the current for a brief moment, no more water comes by, and when the water that has already come by has disappeared, we see the ground, the bed of the current of water. In the same way, when we have interrupted the uninterrupted flood of thoughts, when we turn aside the continuous outpouring, like the surge of a torrent, of perpetual thoughts, we have something like emptiness, but it is not the emptiness of vacuity. It is rather the emptiness in question when we say, for example, that "the temple is empty of monks."

And so, suddenly we have emptiness when we halt what our inner discourse has filled. When we succeed in prolonging this instant of emptiness, at some moment or another we shall have the experience of the qualities of knowledge and clarity that define consciousness.

If, then, we have our eyes closed, we have a view of a kind of disagreeable redness. And if we open our eyes, we may see vivid colors before us, and these can be unsettling. But if we see nothing of a particular color, perhaps even in the absence of all visual perception, the experience will have its utility and will slowly permit us to understand what is meant by a "simple experience of knowledge and clarity."

Emptiness, as well, can be a support for concentration. In this case, one can take the mind itself as subject, or substrate of particularities, or, again, a phenomenon endowed with a form, or, again, the simple sensation of the "I": here we have good objects for analysis of emptiness.

Once we have chosen a suitable object as substrate, we must concentrate our analysis on it. When we have analyzed it to see whether it really exists, we shall ultimately conceive that it is deprived of all essence. Then there will be an emptiness of absence, the emptiness that follows refutation, insubstantiality. Next, when we have arrived at the intellectual conclusion that it is empty from every standpoint, and that this conclusion is a certainty, we must remain perfectly concentrated on this certainty. So much for the "quest of meditation."

One first practices quietude upon a conventional object of concentration. When one has gotten this far, the "quest of the view" —the analysis of the situation in a deep meditative state—begins. This is how one proceeds in the sutras.

In the lower tantras, one practices *samadhi*[21] during "yoga with signs."[22] An individual who has not yet arrived at quietude will accomplish it during yoga with signs and during the recollection that integrates quietude and higher vision into the direct knowledge of emptiness, during "yoga without signs."[23] In the Unsurpassable Tantras, quietude is practiced during the phase of creation,[24] unless the one has already reached it in another way.

MEDITATIVE AND LOGICAL REFUTATION

So much for the matter of quietude. What is the main object of the exercise of quietude? Buddhists interested in liberation practice quietude to attain to the higher vision that knows things directly as they are. And for this direct vision of emptiness to be produced, one must have the view of direct knowledge of emptiness.[25] Without this view, it is impossible for the higher vision of the direct knowledge of the nature of a thing to follow the pure and simple annihilation of this thing.

Now when we speak of emptiness, of what "emptiness" are we speaking? Generally speaking, emptiness of real, or in-itself, existence, the very object of refutation. Among objects of refutation, there are those that are refuted by practicing upon the way and those that are refuted by reasoning. The former are eliminated by means of meditation upon the way and are distinct from the objects of logical refutation, as when one explains emptiness.

How does logical refutation operate here? It demonstrates the nonexistence of the object of refutation. This object has never existed. But then, someone will say, if it has never existed, it will be unnecessary to refute it. Now, by mistake, one is believing in the very thing that does not exist, and from this belief arise the attachment and hatred that have the power to make us experience suffering. The producing cause of suffering, then, consists in attachment and hatred, whose cause is realistic belief: to eliminate this belief, the only means is to eliminate distorted consciousnesses. But this will be accomplished only by declaring them bad.

When, for example, there is danger that an ill-intentioned person is lurking in the dark, we warn one another to take care. It is useless to keep repeating that there is no reason to fear. Once it has actually been verified that there is no reason to fear, the fear provoked by the doubt disappears of itself.

Next, to eliminate naive realism, which is a distorted consciousness, one must be certain that the object does not exist as realism would have it. Such a belief then loses its strength naturally and will disappear little by little with meditation. Nor is this the result only of a logical refutation.

It is by force of habit, and by an inborn belief, that we are subtly convinced that objects are substances—and it is this conviction that deprives us of a just foundation. If we come to the certitude that nothing exists in itself, we shall deliver ourselves from the blind destruction caused by our fixation on a substance.

One cannot deny the existence of the object of refutation, but this refutation must be repeated in thought until this object as substance ceases.[26] We shall refute its real existence by becoming well aware of the difficulties of such an existence, and shall understand that the object of the refutation has never really existed.

That a thing does not exist in itself is the very proof of its unreality.[27]

Questions and Answers V

■ ■ ■ ■

If the clear light of consciousness is constituted of impermanent instants, how can we recall the past?

Consciousness proceeds from instant to instant even on the level of the gross consciousnesses. Yesterday's consciousness no longer exists today, and what happened yesterday is today no more than a memory within the same continuum.

From the fact that each instant is impermanent, at the moment of death, at the last dissolution, only the clear light remains. Is the clear light itself fraught with past tendencies and karma?

We have seen that there is a terrain on which occasional tendencies are deposited, and a terrain on which durable tendencies are deposited. The terrain of the durable tendencies is the simple sensation of the "I," and it is upon this sensation that our reflection will bear. When the innate original clear light is manifested as the wisdom that directly knows emptiness, it can in no case form the terrain of the tendencies, and the tendencies are deposited upon the simple sensation of the "I." But if I seek this "I," I cannot find it. Nor can I find the clear light, since its name is relative to its parts.

The Discernment of the Center and Periphery[1] discusses three absolute levels: the absolute of fact, the absolute that one obtains, and the absolute that one accomplishes. In the tantras the clear light is called the "phase of perfection[2] in absolute truth." In chapter 18 of his *Treasure of the Magic Gem*, Longchen Rabjampa[3] proposes manifold ways of classifying the two fundamental truths, and one of them is this: the original and the innate issue from the absolute truth, and the momentary from the relative. He proclaims the absolute truth, then, of the innate original state, empty of momentary phenomena. He establishes the absolute truth of the innate original clear light. When one compares the suceeding texts that discuss the absolute, one will see that there is one manner of understanding it that is valid for the way of the sutras and another that is valid for the way of the tantras.

What does *emptiness* designate in a tantra like the *Wheel of Time*[4]? We must be able to extract a meaning from each of these texts. Beware of amalgams! Once one pronounces the words *emptiness* and *absolute,* one has the impression of speaking of the same thing, in fact of the absolute. If emptiness must be explained through the use of just one of these two terms, there will be confusion. I must say this; otherwise you might think that the innate original clear light as absolute truth really exists.

What do you think of vegetarianism?

It is wonderful. We must absolutely promote vegetarianism. And even if, when we are at home we cannot be perfectly vegetarian, when we give a reception or have a banquet it is definitely better to offer only vegetarian dishes. Some call themselves vegetarians and consider fish and other animals as vegetables. When one claims to be a vegetarian, one must regard crabs and the other fruits of the sea as meat. *Vegetarian* means "eating only vegetables." Nowadays there are those who call themselves vegetarians, but when they go to a restaurant, you should see how the fish and crabs look at them with big, round eyes!

Can devotion be a way, even the *way, for certain disciples?*

Devotion is essential for the genesis of a special realization. But with devotion alone, things are very difficult. It is important to meditate on all sorts of subjects.

Can anger be beneficial in changing a negative situation?

In principle, anger motivated by compassion is acceptable. We hear of compassion as causal motivation and anger as temporal motivation. The tantras explain how to make anger into a way. So it can be positive. Nevertheless, in the text of the Vehicle of the Bodhisattvas, it is absolutely forbidden to allow oneself to become angry. I am always asked this kind of question. When we have just sustained a dreadful fright, it is better to express our discomfort, even if it has the appearance of anger! In general, unless one methodically applies its antidote to a mounting anger, the anger can only swell more and more. One must see a drawback in it, a problem; as it reveals itself to be indeed out of place, it gradually loses its strength.

You have said that it is intention that determines karma. Does this intention come from karma?

Why not? Is it a fact, for example, that there are negative emotions in the mind that obeys karma? Perhaps. Let us take, however, the case of a person who, in another life, had killed. Born once more into this life, he loves to kill. This urge to kill comes from schemata conditioned by the great habit he had of killing.

You have said that the number of continuums of consciousness that constitute individuals has neither increased nor decreased. Do you mean that their number is definite, or rather that it is infinite—that they cannot be counted?

They cannot be counted.

Yesterday you said that the form and color of a flower come from karma, but I thought I had understood that karma concerns only animate beings endowed with a consciousness. A flower has no consciousness. Then how can you explain that its color and form are results of karma?

A person who loves flowers of all colors, and who has a garden with many flowers in it, owes that in large part to the strength of projection of his or her karma. A flower has no sensations entailed by its form and its color. An individual who enjoys the flower, however, including the insect that lives within it, experiences the effects of the functioning of the causes and conditions that permit enjoyment of the flower, and this has a relationship with the karma of the animate being itself.

Indeed this is why the form of the world, for example, under its general aspect, is the way it is in relation to the karma common to those who live in it. Consequently, there is a relationship with karma for all the components of the landscape, like forests, flowers, deserts. Of what nature is this relationship? This is an enigma. I think that the world is constituted, roughly speaking, of four elements. The five internal elements [earth, water, fire, air, and space] are further divided into gross and subtle. The deepest and most subtle of the elements has bonds with the clear light. So there is a connection from that side. This appears in the *Great Commentary of the Wheel of Time* of Mipham Rinpoche.[5] With the exception of this point, the other relationships are not evident.

The world around us is a projection of universal karma. I believe that its most subtle particularities obey the laws of nature studied in biology and chemistry. At present, for example, things are differentiated: we distinguish the animate from the inanimate. A flower is not a body; there is a difference. If we go back to the particles of the "big bang," we do not find, right after the big bang, a particle "tagged" to be flesh, nor particles for flowers, for rocks, and so on. *The Tantra of the Wheel of Time* speaks of "particles of space," a kind of particle that, in my opinion, must have been present at the moment of the big bang. I believe that this type of particle diversified in the course of evolution into particles for making rocks, flowers, and flesh, in cooperation with karma. Indeed, physicists explain that, at the beginning, the particles were extremely subtle and very little differentiated. I do not know their exact names. In any case, here we have things of extreme subtlety.

You have said that ignorance is inherent in the continuum, and that the continuum has no beginning. It would seem, then, that ignorance will have no end, because the continuum has none.

While ignorance can be prevented from lasting, it is impossible to block consciousness. Likewise, the individual cannot be prevented from being. The opposite of ignorance is wisdom. Ignorance, unlike wisdom, has no logical support. In the course of this life alone, for instance, our consciousness always is, but anger, let us say, sometimes arises and sometimes dies away. If we meditate a great deal on love in order to work against anger, the anger will gradually lose its strength. At the moment of death, it is only the consciousness of this life that disappears. Death is not the complete annihilation of consciousness. There is a way to prevent hatred, but nothing can stop consciousness.

You often speak of the five aggregates. What are they?

Forms, sensations, perceptions, compositions,[6] and the consciousnesses.

What is the difference between the continuum of the clear light and a particle in space?

A particle in space has a form—a subtle form, surely, but a form. The clear light is consciousness. A particle in space has no beginning, and I do not know whether it has an end—perhaps not. Why? Animate beings are infinite. If they have no end, they will never stop. If their projects have no end, their flow can never stop. Infinite, unlimited: it is so difficult to envisage the end.

If all human beings become buddhas, what will happen?

There will be a great celebration.

In the face of so much violence and abuse, is nonviolence the only possible response?

I believe so. One can always respond that violence calls for counterviolence, and then there is no end of violence. I say that our century [the twentieth century] is the century of violence, and that, if we all set ourselves to it, the coming century could be the century of dialogue.

The Path to Ultimate Omniscience

■ ■ ■ ■

On the basis of the Four Noble Truths and the two fundamental truths, we have come to the refuge. At this point, it remains for us to go from the refuge to ultimate omniscience, the dignity of the Conqueror.[1] This path has three steps: avoiding non-meritorious acts, in other words evil; eliminating the negative emotions; and effacing the habitual schemata imprinted by the negative emotions.

Let us move to an explanation of the second step, eliminating the negative emotions. This step consists in meditating on transcendent knowledge, on the basis of discipline and by means of quietude, in order to arrive at direct knowledge of insubstantiality. We must therefore establish the meaning of insubstantiality.

THE MEANING OF INSUBSTANTIALITY

All Buddhist philosophers agree that it is because of ignorance that we turn in the circle of deaths and rebirths. But why is this necessarily the reason?

No one among us wishes to suffer. What we—all of us—wish naturally is to be happy. Now, one would say that we work almost voluntarily to create the causes of our suffering, which is the effect of a certain confusion. Without this confusion, we could create the causes of the happiness to which we aspire. What we wish is to be happy, but we work against the causes of happiness precisely because of our confusion. This being the case, our existence is subjected to the sufferings of samsara, and it is taught that the cause of samsara is none other than ignorance. Ignorance, then, has the power to create samsara.

As for identifying this ignorance, just as there are more or less subtle theses on insubstantiality, there are more or less subtle explanations of ignorance. To end ignorance, one must attack it with the help of a state of mind whose mode of perception will be contrary to it. A state of mind whose mode is not contrary will only attack indirectly what ought to be abolished.

Consequently, Chandrakirti can write: "Since love, for example, is not contrary to confusion, it cannot abrogate very evil acts." In other words, on the basis of the fact that love and compassion do not necessarily apprehend things by contradicting confusion, they cannot mount a frontal assault on it.

In his *Four Hundred Stanzas*, Aryadeva writes:

Becoming's germ is consciousness,
And its field of activity, the objects of consciousness.
When the insubstantiality of these objects is perceived,
The germ of becoming is blocked.

In other words, if one reduces to consciousness in general this consciousness that is the seed of becoming, then as long as there is consciousness, one will have to remain in the circle of deaths and rebirths. In order to halt samsara, consciousness would have to cease, but that would be contrary to the texts of Nagarjuna—and contrary to the facts besides.

There is a particular consciousness, then, the consciousness that goes along with substantialist ignorance, that maintains us in the circle of existences. To refute the substantialist ignorance, which functions as the seed of existences, it is necessary to recognize the insubstantiality of the objects perceived as substances precisely by reason of this ignorance. Then, consciousness as the seed of existences will desist.

But, if objects must be held insubstantial, what is this substantiality that they are missing?

The *Four Hundred Stanzas* once more:

What exists dependently
Is hardly independent.
Now all of this is not independent;
Then all is insubstantial.

So any phenomenon existing in interdependence is not an independent entity. Now, because none of the phenomena designated by the self and the aggregates exists independently, they are all called "empty of substantial existence." Here it must be understood that the thing to refute is the concept of independence, independent existence. It is this "independence" that all the Madhyamikas point to as the thing to be refuted in a general way.

When one enters into the details, as we have seen, it is on this precise point that the three masters, beginning with Buddhapalita, have expressed themselves with the most clarity. Buddhapalita's commentary on Nagarjuna's *Fundamental Treatise* was criticized by Bhavaviveka. Then these criticisms of certain points of terminology and interpretation were answered by Chandrakirti, who clarified each of the points.

What is it, then, that clearly emerges from these three masters' refutations, affirmations, objections, and counterobjections?

Bhavaviveka and his successors have shown that, in a certain middle way, what we presently perceive as forms and other phenomena, these appearances of independent realities, do indeed exist on the conventional level, as if they had an objective existence.

It is the nature of these appearances that the three masters call independent reality, existing reality. The mind that perceives these independent realities is not in error with respect to essentially real appearances. What do they mean by that? That these "independent" realities exist perfectly well on the conventional level.

By contrast, for Buddhapalita and Chandrakirti this kind of independent reality does not exist at all, so to perceive it is an error. On the one side we hear of true knowledge, and on the other of a mistake. This shows how they define the object of refutation, and we perceive that there is a difference of subtlety in the object that each side refutes.

Within the Middle Way, then, some assert an independent reality on the conventional level, and others do not. It would be better, however, that there be no logical criticism of the view we are presently explaining, which denies the independent reality of everything, even at the conventional level. We can examine this view all we wish, and we shall still find no absurdity in the refusal to admit, in conventional truth, any independent reality at all. And it is even possible to demonstrate, in all logic, that this is the ultimate thought of Nagarjuna and his successor Buddhapalita.

When we reflect on what remains once we have refuted the existence of independent realities on the conventional level alone, it is not uncommon to experience a sense of nihilism. In Nagarjuna's *Fundamental Treatise,* we find the realists' criticisms addressed to the Madhyamikas, which say, in substance: You claim that all phenomena are naturally empty, or empty [of being] in themselves. If all phenomena are naturally empty, each of them empty in essence, nothing will any longer be able to exist. Each phenomenon will lack an essence and attributes. Your philosophy, then, is only a great nihilism.

Such is the objection of the realists of the Lesser Vehicle, who continue as follows: For example, you refute the four modes of possible production.[2] You say that the real refers neither to being nor to nonbeing—that it is free from all conceptual constructions tied up with being and nonbeing.[3] You are in danger of having nothing on your mind but a pure nothingness!

Here is what Nagarjuna responds:

When the Madhyamikas comment on the ultimate intention of the Conqueror, they speak of "nonexistence in itself" for the sole reason that things are produced in interdependence, and that they therefore do not exist in themselves. They do not say that, since they absolutely do not exist, it is contrary to their essence to exist.

We can read in the *Fundamental Treatise* that what is produced in interdependence cannot exist by sole reason of its essence; that what cannot exist by essence is empty of substantiality; and that what is empty of substantiality is called empty, naturally empty. Consequently, what is empty of substantiality exists only and solely in dependence. In the expression "dependent designation," *dependent* means "not autonomous": what depends on something else is not autonomous. And the limit of eternal being disappears. Considering that that does not produce itself in autonomous fashion, we speak of "designation." And neither will what exists as designation be held as pure nothingness.

But a dependent designation is absolutely without any reality in itself. It is a matter of an entity that does not have autonomous existence but that is not purely nonexistent either. Thus, it is not denied that it has an action obedient to causality and producing positive and negative effects. What exists as designation, without, however, its activity existing in itself either is a dependent reality.

This is how the Madhyamikas perceive things. Such is the

Middle Way. As clearly emerges from Chandrakirti's *Introduction to the Middle Way,* and in conformity with the author's commentary on his work, it is impossible to know perfectly the insubstantiality of the individual as long as one does not directly know the insubstantiality of phenomena. This is the teaching, nor is the difference a matter of subtlety. *The Jeweled Necklace*[4] says:

> As long as belief in the reality of the aggregates endures,
> Belief will endure in the reality of the "I."

In other words, until one acquires the strength to refute the objects of attachment of naive realism, for which the aggregates are real, the realism that has as its object the individual self will be perpetuated. The individual self of which the Svatantrikas and the lower schools speak is only the gross aspect of the self. The insubstantiality of the individual self, in brief, designates the fact that no absolutely independent individual exists, and the insubstantiality of phenomena designates the fact that the aggregates, for example, just as all phenomena, do not really exist.

Direct knowledge of the insubstantiality of the individual self and direct knowledge of the insubstantiality of phenomena mount a frontal assault on belief in reality, or the realism that consists in attaching itself to the individual as to a self, the realism that consists of attaching itself to the aggregates as if they really existed.

In what order do these two realisms appear? The realistic ignorance that consists in believing in the real existence of the aggregates forms the basis on which the realism that consists in believing in the reality of the individual develops.

When the "I" presents itself to the mind, it is the aggregates constituting the basis of designation of the "I" that present themselves as the mind's object. Is it not then that we feel ourselves to be an "I"? I am not sure that this is always valid for direct knowledge of insubstantiality, but generally speaking it is often somewhat easier to establish the insubstantiality of the individual from the very fact of his or her substrate.[5] We begin, then, by considering the individual self. The insubstantiality of phenomena follows.

EXISTENCE AND REAL EXISTENCE

Are form and the other phenomena refuted by reasoning during meditation? No. What does reasoning refute? It refutes the existence in itself of form and the other phenomena. Still, for one who directly knows the nature of form and the other phenomena, the one for whom emptiness is a certainty, form and the other phenomena do not appear. These things cease.

The mind that analyzes the nature of form and the other phenomena seeks their nature alone. The mind that seeks the real mode of form and of the other phenomena finds none of these phenomena. These things that have the appearance of form and the other phenomena do not exist in a real mode. And so, in the mind of the person who seeks their real mode, or knows it with certitude, these things do not appear. That is the whole story. Which does not mean that form and the other phenomena have ceased, or that they have been denied.

Visual consciousness, for example, does not perceive sounds. There is no question of doubting a sound under the pretext that visual consciousness has not heard it. Visual consciousness perceives only form. Visual consciousness is not the consciousness that apprehends sound. One cannot explain the nonexistence of a sound, then, by positing that visual consciousness does not perceive the sound. Sound is the exclusive object of auditory consciousness, which apprehends sound. It cannot be the object of visual consciousness.

Likewise, the mind concentrated on an analysis of the real

mode of things does not perceive things that do not exist in a real mode. To say that this person does not perceive them is not to say that he or she perceives their nonexistence. It is because they cannot be the objects of his or her perception that this person does not perceive them. And so, for the reason that examines their real mode, form and the other phenomena are but undiscoverable objects, which does not imply their negation pure and simple, or the discovery of their nonexistence.

I was asked this question the other day. When all constructions of the concept are perfectly laid to rest during contemplation in the space of this perfect laying-to-rest, they are not perceived, they do not appear in this dimension, and that is the whole story. Which does not imply that the constructions of the concept do not exist.

One may read in *Journey Toward the Awakening*[6] that it is not possible to refute form, sound, or the other phenomena, or indeed the consciousnesses that respectively apprehend them. It is the content of thought, says Shantideva, the concept of real existence, which is precisely the cause of suffering, that must be refuted, and not the consciousnesses of form and sound and so on or these objects themselves.

Then what is denied? The concept of, or belief in, their real existence, which is the cause of suffering—that is what is denied. There is a distinction to be made, then, between existing and really existing.

What is "existence"? Only a name. As for "real existence," this is "objective" existence."[7] When an object is presented to us, it is hardly its nominal existence that appears to us, but its objective existence.

Meanwhile, it is possible to think that, when the mind apprehends these phenomena, they exist as they appear. And it is possible to think the contrary. It is even possible to apprehend them think-

ing that they are really as they appear. Until they have been analyzed in consistent fashion, they seem to exist objectively.

Take these flowers, for example, of which it could be thought
that they are white. In that case, one thinks simply that they are
white, and not that they are objective as they appear. There is an
appearance of flowers, and this simple apparition confers on them
a kind of objective existence. Indeed, we perceive them as bases of
designation, or objects. But with the exception of direct and
immediate knowledge of emptiness, all perceptions are illusory.

What is meant by this? That apart from the direct knowledge of
emptiness, all states of mind for which phenomena appear as
objectively existing are distorted thoughts or consciousnesses. And
it is under this aspect that it is said that it is entirely mistaken.

We can find these flowers pretty and become attached to them.
We shall become attached in mind to finding them objectively
beautiful, and belief in their reality will emerge. In the mind apprehending the flowers, there is the exclusive thought of the flowers,
which appear as if endowed with objective existence. Now, with
the fact of believing that anything is objective and perfectly independent, there it is, naive realism.

At first there is an instant of perception that does not differentiate between real and unreal—the simple perception that consists
of being conscious of the flowers. Next, when one experiences a
slight attachment to these flowers, when one says to oneself that
there is an independent object here that arouses attachment and—
the attachment proves it—merits attachment, there is no escape
from ascribing it the particularity of being real. There it is, naive
realism.

Finally, when these flowers are seen by someone who has a
good general understanding of the fact that phenomena do not
really exist, he or she perceives them as existing objectively, and by
simple reason of the fact that they exist objectively only at the level

of appearance, this person will think that, even if they therefore seem to exist really, this is scarcely the case. This is apprehension of flowers to which will be given the particularity of not being real.

It is possible, then, to apprehend these flowers in three ways: first, without conferring on them the particularity of being real or not; second, judging them real; and third, having had the direct experience of emptiness, perceiving them from the standpoint of their unreality.

Existence is purely nominal, and nothing has ever had objective existence. Furthermore, as this existence can have good or bad effects, there must certainly be something that produces these effects. But it remains absolutely impossible to put one's finger on this something. This something is strictly undiscoverable. It is a matter not at all of nothingness but of nothing that would objectively exist. Absolutely in no way. And it will be said that things exist by virtue of the fact of their name, precisely without meriting it.

The word *simple,* in the expression "simple designation," does not mean that the only realities are names. It does not mean that there are only names and not objects. There must be an object suited to the name. A name can be wrong. If realities were names and nothing else, it would be unnecessary, it seems to me, to amuse oneself by seeing if these names corresponded to their objects. There are objects, objects that are not names, and although they are present, one can say nothing about them. There exists an object corresponding to a name. Even if it exists, what is its essence? Only a name. It is an unnameable object whose existence is owing to a name—nothing that objectively exists.

This mode of existence, which is not the simple nonexistence of the object, is existence on the strength of a name, a conventional designation, nothing but a being produced by the power of designation inherent in a concept. But it is nothing that could exist objectively. And given this fact, when we wish to know what object is being spoken of in terms of objective existence, this object turns out to be undiscoverable. There, then, is what must be understood when it is said that things do not exist by the sole fact of their essence.

The Madhyamikas-Svatantrikas admit this objective existence. For them it is a simple name, but, as I have said, it does not designate a simple nominal existence without anything objective. They consider that what appears as an objective, independent reality to a sound consciousness—in other words to a consciousness unsullied by momentary causes of error[8]—exists. That which appears exists by essence on the conventional level as objective reality. Because this appearance is the perception of a sound consciousness, the non-Prasangikas see in it something that exists objectively, and independently of its designation.

In brief, if things could exist on their own, we should have to envisage, for example, that a real Matthew exists to whom the name of Matthew corresponds. Let us imagine, then, an independent reality that we shall call Matthew. Afterwards, we can have the thought "Father Matthew is here." This thought will be in conformity with its object. If, independently of the designation Matthew, and without the existence of the word *Matthew* because of the fact of its apparition to a sound consciousness, this name had somehow an extraordinary existence,[9] then someone who does not know Matthew's name would need simply to see Matthew in order to know his name. But this is not the case. Something appears as if it existed objectively and by essence. A name is attached to this appearance, and it is this union of methods and knowledge that enables the appearance to be posited as an existent phenomenon. And this is how, for the Svatantrikas, phenomena exist.[10]

For the Prasangikas, the difference is the following. Existence is a strictly nominal thing and in no case objective. The texts of the

Middle Way always use the comparison of the rope and the serpent. In the half–light a speckled rope, rolled up, lies on the ground. Someone might think it is a serpent, but the serpent that this person imagines will not have the least existence. There has never been a serpent "in" this spotted rope. In the same way, it is more than the aggregates that impose the thought of the self.

When one interprets the aggregates to be the individual, then in this object to which the thought "I am" or "here is an individual" is added, there has never been the slightest possibility of actually being an individual. Just as in the spotted rope there has never been the slightest element constituting a serpent, and even if the notion of the individual, formed on the basis of the aggregates, does correspond to a true knowing, the sure nonexistence of the serpent in the rope is analogous to the sure nonexistence of the individual in the aggregates.

But the thought that there is a serpent when there is only a rope is a distorted perception, but the thought that the aggregates are the locus of the individual is not an erroneous knowing. What is the difference, then? We cannot say that there is a serpent where there is a rope, nor can we say that there is an individual where there are aggregates. And this for the good reason that the perception of a serpent in place of a rope can be contradicted by another perception on the conventional level: only bring some light, and the idea that it is a matter of a rope and not of a serpent will impose itself as a true idea in the conventional sense. It is certain that when we extend a hand, we shall touch a rope and not a serpent. This kind of conventional evidence is adequate to contradict the mistake, and in that it is not erroneous.

By contrast, the idea that there is an individual where there are aggregates can be proved false by no other conventional reason. To the regard of someone else, there will also be an individual. From the buddhas all the way down to us ordinary beings, we hear of nothing but that there are individuals, and not individuals that are somehow extracted from the aggregates. It is not totally false to think that an individual exists on the basis of the aggregates. However, it comes to the same thing to say—if the thought that the individual draws its existence from the aggregates is not a false idea—that where there are aggregates there are individuals but where there is a rope there is no serpent.

Then what is the difference? It must be explained that, from the viewpoint of the subject, consciousness, the true knowing of another person will abolish the idea of a serpent in place of the rope; but the thought that conceives an individual on the basis of the aggregates cannot be abolished by another intelligence on the conventional level; and, in this context, we have a nonerroneous consciousness in accord with its object. No difference, then, in terms of objective nonexistence.

The "mistake" arises from another viewpoint. That the thought "Here is an individual" would have the appearance of reality is a mistake. But the perception of this consciousness is not yet affected by realistic belief. It is only the thought that there is an individual here. The object of this perception is the individual, and no other true conventional cognition will be able to prove the contrary. This consciousness mistakes in perceiving a real existence. The object of this perception is the individual, and in that it is correct. It is belief in someone real, then, that constitutes the mistake.

Consequently, the consciousness that perceives a rope as a serpent is held to be a distortion. It is an illusion. The belief that an individual exists on the basis of the aggregates is an error, but this belief is in accord with its object. Unless one manages to see the difference, one is in serious danger of thinking that, for the Prasangikas, good and bad acts do not have positive and negative consequences, since they do not have any veritable reality. The

Prasangikas differentiate between a person seen in a dream and one in flesh and blood.

They regard it as necessary to be able to define everything that—on the conventional level—is authentic or not, a criterion of true knowledge or not. But it is absolutely impossible to define a criterion of true knowledge on the sole basis of the object. It is to common sense, then, that one has recourse to posit what is true or false in terms of knowledge; and one must likewise have recourse to common sense to know whether something exists or not, whether it is authentic or not. For the Prasangikas, then, all phenomena are but conceptual designations. And conceptual designations are only that.

Are these simple conceptual designations my own thoughts? Her thoughts? The thoughts of the animate beings of the universe? We can never know. And the fact that we say that they are only conceptual designations is itself but a conceptual designation. There is no escaping it. What exists utterly simply, merely in thought—that too is but a conceptual postulate. Then, satisfied with appearances alone, we classify all phenomena as samsara and nirvana in terms of their appearance. If you wish me to define them for you, I shall say that they exist for common sense by the very fact of their names.

But when, not overwhelmed by mere appearance, you analyze the real condition, or real existence, of these phenomena, you enter upon an analysis of their absolute truth, and then you cannot find anything. Contemporary physics explains that we can posit nothing as a reality when we reach a very subtle level. Is there not a similarity here with the Buddhist approach to the absolute truth of phenomena?

When they analyze objects provided with a form, a shape, certain scientists seem to be able to find nothing, and they propose that these objects appear only to the mind. We cannot help thinking of the view of the Chittamatrins. Some researchers think that the mind exists really, that it is concrete. How far is this from Chittamatra?

The Prasangika position appears again in the *Journey Toward the Awakening*. Objects, on the outside, as well as the subject, on the inside, seem to have no real existence but only a conventional existence.

As for demonstrating the unreality of the individual "I," I shall rest content with evoking it through a citation from the *Jeweled Necklace:*

Human beings are not earth, are not water,
Are not fire, nor air, nor space,
Nor consciousness. If they are none of all this,
If they are other, what are human beings?

If human beings are the gathering of six elements,
They are not really human beings. Just so,
If they designate the gathering of six elements,
They do not exist by essence.

EXAMINING CAUSES AND EFFECTS

At this point, in order to demonstrate the insubstantiality of phenomena, we shall admit that certain things exist by essence. To prove that there are independent realities, we shall explain that they arise from causes, that they can produce effects, that they have an essence, and that this essence is in conformity with their attributes.

And the other way around, to demonstrate that a reality has no essence, we shall prove that it arises from a cause and not from itself, for what proceeds from a cause does not exist by essence. If the phenomenon of production really existed, things would have to arise from themselves, or from something else, or from both at once, or from no cause. There is no fifth possibility.

That things arise from themselves, or from the Self, is the Samkhya thesis. In Samkhya, causes and effects all have the nature of *pradhana*[11] alone. They all present themselves as the expression, or manifestation, of *pradhana*. Whatever the nature of the effect, it will be the same as the nature of the cause. As we examine this identical nature of effects and causes, we shall distinguish manifest effects from nonmanifest effects. In short, the moment there is a cause, the effect has, so to speak, collected all of its attributes. In this case, as far as the object is concerned, during the productive phase of the effect, the effect already exists the moment the cause exists. If it must arise a second time since the beginning, then this origination will not be one, which is absurd.

To "arise," in our sense, is to appear as a novelty, something that did not exist before and that is not constituted with the help of causes and conditions. If something already exists at the moment of the cause that is going to engender it, it will no longer be necessary for its production to be the emergence of a novelty. The error, then, is in this meaningless production. If what already is did not have to arise anew, this would go on forever. The idea also is in error, then, in proposing a production that will never finish.

Let us move on, now, to what is called production starting from something else. For Bhavaviveka, things arise from other things not solely on the absolute level but also on the relative level, where they arise from causes different from themselves.

The Prasangikas speak of "production starting from four alternatives," when it is a matter of proving the real existence of production. When we speak of something "else," we cannot admit that its otherness is a pure abstraction. We begin, then, by imagining an "other" that would be perfectly independent. If we are told that an effect springs from a cause that is other, real, and independent, then at the moment of the seed its product, the sprout, does not yet exist.

If, then, we speak of an independent "other" when we consider the sprout and the seed, we shall have two independent and real phenomena, different from each other. We can say that they are different in accordance with their reciprocal position. It is in thought alone that something that belongs not to the present but to the future, or to the past, can be considered "other." But then the difference will be purely nominal, for nothing can exist that would be other *and* independent. At the moment of the producing seed, then, the produced effect does not yet exist. Indeed, this is why the one exists only in relationship with the other, and why the designation "other" is impossible.

And this is how the four Buddhist schools of philosophy explain that, at the moment of the process of production, the cause approaching cessation and the effect approaching origination are simultaneous. At the moment when the effect approaches origination, it must exist. The origination of what? The origination of the effect. In this origination of the effect, the effect is the support and the origination is the supported, the effect is the substrate of the qualities and the origination is a quality. Now, if the support and the supported exist independently—since without the existence of the support, which is the effect, the origination is impossible—then when the supported, or the origination, exists, the support, or the effect, will have to exist as well.

At the moment when the cause approaches cessation and the effect origination, the effect does not exist. Thus there is no origination. And so, origination starting from another is not the right solution either. Therefore it is taught that origination, or production, is also indefensible. It is not possible to maintain, then, in the idea of production starting from something else, either the idea of the other thing or the idea of production.

Next, when we examine the "I" with the help of the sevenfold reasoning [of Chandrakirti][12] it is impossible to posit a being existing by virtue of the very fact of its essence. The reasonings on being, nonbeing, production, and cessation show that if something existed by essence, no cause could create it. If it were in the essence of a thing not to exist, no cause could produce it and it could produce no effect.

In sum, interdependent production deals with relative existence in terms of the bonds of interdependence. The relative and the non relative are opposites, and there is no third alternative: either there is relative production or we are in the absolute. What exists in a relative manner is empty of absolute existence. There is no reality existing in absolute fashion.

The essential is to reflect by oneself, according to one's own personal experience, then to meditate. Appearances will continue to present themselves, as they always have, but if, in reflection, one has arrived at the least comprehension of the mode of being of phenomena, the phenomena will gradually present themselves in another manner.

And so the thoughts accompanying naive realism will relax their grasp, and one will pass through a series of states of consciousness that are no longer necessarily conditioned by realism. Steeped in the idea of renunciation, these states of consciousness lead to the meditation that unites quietude and higher vision in the direct knowledge of emptiness. Thus they are causes of the attainment of liberation. They will form the very way of liberation.

When, steeped in the spirit of Awakening, we meditate, in the union of quietude and higher vision that directly knows insubstantiality, we hold the direct antidote to the cognitive veil, and that antidote allows us to attain omniscience. As a consequence, if we can meditate on the state of very subtle consciousness designated by the direct knowledge of emptiness, we shall make short work of the dissipation of the cognitive veil. And this is the effect of the special depth of the tantras.

This is the end of the Buddhist lecture properly so called. All of these things I have approached roughly, in their germ. I do not know the subject very well either. In any case, consult the texts constantly. By combining what you will have learned there and your experience, you will gradually gain an idea of what it is all about.

As for the vow of the spirit of Awakening this afternoon, we shall have to respect the concepts of master and disciple. It is desirable, then, that only those come who have examined me well. Since last year, I say that they should have a kind of card [of fidelity].

May I ask the adepts of Shoukden not to join us.

Questions and Answers VI

■ ■ ■ ■

Is it possible to love without attachment?

Yes. This is what one should do. It is important to make a careful distinction. Attachment is full of partiality [or bias]. It is full of mental projections. Compassion is impartial and ignores mental projections.

You have spoken of emotions that obscure, but is there an emotion that dispels ignorance?

There are two kinds of emotions. Love, compassion, unselfishness, all of that, those are positive emotions. As we become used to them, we can develop them endlessly. Positive emotions help knowledge. That is hardly the case with the negative emotions.

Is it possible for persons who are not enlightened to lead others to the Awakening?

They cannot lead them to the very end. Instinctively, they will tell them to act in this way or that, and so on. If they wish to be guides, they must take their inspiration from their own experience. And even if this experience is not complete, they will say: "Do this," and so forth. Ha, ha! For that matter, this is my case. I practice somewhat things like meditation on the spirit of Awakening, meditation on emptiness. I have no experience. I have looked at the great texts worthy of trust. "Hasten in this direction," they say. "Hasten in that direction." I guess you could say that this has done me a little good. I do not know that it has done me a great deal.

If there is no ego, what is it that justifies compassion?

We say only that there is no really existing "I," not at all that the "I" as simple name does not exist. You have not always made the distinction between something that does not *really* exist and something that does not exist at all. Still, when it is said that "belief in personhood is the springboard[1] of buddhahood," what is meant is our wandering in samsara. Now, when one embarks upon the way, it is precisely because of this conviction, which makes one believe strongly in the real existence of the "I," that one says: "If *I* deliver *myself* from suffering, if *I* attain happiness," and so on. This belief in personhood is scarcely a bad thing. The masters are accustomed to explain that it is like the springboard that permits the attainment of the state of a buddha.

The teachings of the secret Mantras are profound, then, but until one has assembled all the conditions permitting meditation on these teachings, one will make solid progress in holding to the way of the sutras. Likewise, the teachings of the Prasangikas, such as the fact that no phenomenon exists by essence, are the most profound. Still, unless one can accept this kind of philosophy, unless it suits one's form of intelligence, one will make solid progress in holding to the philosophy of the Svatantrikas or to that of the Chittamatrins.

How does compassion arise from emptiness and the shining continuum of the mind?

Compassion denotes many things. There are many ways of understanding it. If what we commonly call compassion is impregnated with the knowledge of emptiness, I think that one may visualize the end of suffering. Since there exists a means of arresting suffering, the one afflicted with suffering will all the more have the idea of emerging from it. If there were no means of being delivered from suffering, we would think that there is nothing to be done, even if we do "our best," and despair would result.

There have recently been experiments with cloning. What is the karma of the clones? Are they endowed with consciousness?

If they feel pleasure and pain, and if they have perceptions, we must necessarily say that they have a consciousness, that they have karma. What acts have entailed a similar effect? Only the omniscient one can know directly. We should have much difficulty with doing so. The reasonings on emptiness permit us to understand this kind of thing. We must reflect on it, making use of the logical analysis of their "emptiness." In general, in karmic causality, good attracts good and evil, evil. If we evaluate these things little by little, we shall be able to know them only vaguely. I find this question extremely subtle, and of insurmountable difficulty, as long as the cognitive veil is not dissipated.

How may one surmount a very deep feeling of loneliness?

Whatever the origin of this feeling, it is not without association with one's point of view. Whether or not one has a religious belief, the main reason for this feeling is that, in one's mind, there is too little love. When we have too little love for others, it is our way of seeing things that should be saddled with the blame. We think that others do not love us, and that is why we feel alone.

Why refuse suffering? Is this not a sign of weakness? Is it not proof that we do not accept life in its totality?

If it is possible to be rid of suffering definitively, if the third and fourth noble truths are true, then it is worth the trouble to reflect on the first two. If the first two are false, then there is nothing for it but alcohol and sex, since it will be perfectly useless to try to do anything about one's suffering. If it is impossible to conquer suffering, then it is vain to think about it. I think that, across the board, the goal of life is to be happy.

Are we responsible for our illnesses? Are they our fault?

When we have done everything as far as prevention is concerned, when we have tried all possible therapies, if the illness turns out to be incurable, then it is well to reflect on karmic causality. In Buddhism, we are necessarily responsible, but that does not mean that we ought to accept the suffering. We must try to resolve the suffering by all possible means. It is as if, in order to be delivered from great pain, we were to put up with some little ones.

Why should we work against the emotions? Might we not let them die away of themselves?

We have already spoken of this apropos of anger. But to repeat, there are certain emotions that it is useful to uproot, and there are others that gain in strength, that hold sway, once we tolerate them.

Do people blind from birth have a visual consciousness? When one goes blind and recalls certain images, is that visual consciousness or something else?

I could not say whether it is a matter of visual consciousness. A mental image presents itself to the mind. Regardless, what is meant by "visual consciousness" in the case of someone blind from birth, if this consciousness necessarily depends on the organ of sight? It can be a matter of the awakening of old tendencies. The situation is not the same if these tendencies do not manifest themselves. The difference must be there. The reawakening of old schemata. The subject should be researched.

Can one receive Buddhist teachings while remaining Christian?

I think so. In the first place, you can be Christian, and you can tell yourself that you could be Buddhist. You are happy to have taken refuge in the Buddha; you love Jesus as well. Then you follow each of these religions in their specific points. But when you attain Buddhist emptiness, absolute truth presents certain difficulties.

Practicing the Teachings

■ ■ ■ ■

THE VOW OF THE SPIRIT OF AWAKENING

I am going to speak now of what is called the vow of the spirit of Awakening, with ritual, of the taking of the vow of the votive spirit of Awakening,[1] with promise. If one has exercised oneself in the spirit of Awakening by spiritual training, and if one has the slightest experience of it, this experience will be stabilized if one takes the vow of the votive spirit of Awakening.

There are an incalculable number of rituals, including all sorts of rituals of the spirit of Awakening, that can be extensive and abridged, that is, condensed. Whatever the object of the ritual, I have preferred those that give much to reflect upon in just a few words. I find rituals that are more wordy than thoughtful to be tiresome. Today's ritual, then, will be very brief.

I shall begin with a few words on the spirit of Awakening.

To "produce, or engender, the spirit of Awakening" is to expand one's mind. Up until now we have thought essentially of ourselves, each of us. Let us expand our mind, then, by turning it toward the ensemble of animate beings. And besides doing our best to take on the good of all beings, we shall reflect on the vision of emptiness just explained, as it shows that impurity can be exhausted, and that the truth of cessation is a possibility. And in addition, we shall think of something that can be brought to realization in our psychic continuum.

Accordingly, when we reflect, always for the good of beings, that each one's continuum can receive the vision of emptiness—that it is in fact possible, in each person's continuum, that the truth of cessation can be brought to realization—when we think in this way, and only then, we do not limit ourselves to do our best for beings. But, since it is possible to deliver them from suffering and its cause, we have only to decide to do everything possible for their liberation. We shall proceed in this way, then, having recourse to transcendent knowledge in order to place no limits whatever on the growth of the correct production of the spirit of Awakening.

Animate beings are innumerable, but, like us, each has but one wish—not to suffer, and to be happy. In this we are all alike. Just as we ourselves deserve to be delivered from suffering, all animate beings deserve to be uncoupled from their individual sufferings.

Each of us has our own way of dissipating sufferings, and our own way of realizing happiness, and the same is true for all animate beings. Each "I" is precious and important, but it counts as one only in relation to the beings whose teeming masses touch the confines of space: animate beings are actually infinite in number. The most important thing is the greatest number, as one may read in *Journey Toward the Awakening:*

> Since we all have equal need to be happy,
> What privilege would make of me the single object of my
>   efforts toward happiness?
> And since we all dread
> Danger and suffering,

By what privilege would I have the right to be protected,
I alone and not others?[2]

Given that all of us, others and myself, have an equal need to be happy, Shantideva wonders why he would be the sole object of his efforts for happiness. Likewise, since none of us wishes to suffer, he asks himself how he could dream of finding a means of protecting himself alone from suffering.

But that is not all. There is a very great bond between our happiness and suffering and that of others. Were there absolutely no connection between the happiness and suffering of each one and the happiness and suffering of others, we should be able never to think of the happiness and sufferings of others, and the happiness and suffering of each one would respond to his or her aspirations alone. But this is scarcely the case. If others are happy, our own happiness is possible. If all others are unhappy, it will be difficult for us to be the only happy being.

And, what is more, the more we think of the happiness and suffering of others, the more strength our mind will have. The more we think only of ourselves, the more hopes and apprehensions we shall have, and in the same proportion. Indeed, it is to the extent of our hopes and apprehensions that we shall be afraid or experience great dreads.

We must also cherish ourselves, since, if we have no self-esteem, we cannot esteem the other. We begin by turning this esteem upon ourselves, after which we shall necessarily cherish others.

Still, as far as self-esteem is concerned, thinking really only of ourselves and disdaining the happiness of others makes one unhappy. We shall be unhappy if we are alone in life, and we shall cause unhappiness to our family, if we have one, and unhappiness to society. In a word, for those who think only of themselves and neglect others, cherish themselves and disdain the happiness of others, that is the origin of the problem.

If, on the contrary, we think that the good of others is far more vast than our own good, we shall only find more courage within ourselves, we shall have no regret, we shall be satisfied in mind, and thus shall think that we are good for something. Even in private we shall think that we have accomplished what is necessary in life, and this kind of thought will bring happiness into the heart of our very family. What is truly useful, then, comes from this kind of state of mind; and the esteem we bear the other, cherishing him or her, will contribute to the general good as well as to our personal good. There we have the basis.

Some may wonder whether, in taking on the happiness and suffering of others, in thinking of the suffering of others more than of our own, we shall not add to our own unhappiness. To this, *Journey Toward the Awakening* answers no. When one has a problem oneself and feels distressed, when one has tried everything in vain, one is helpless, cast down, impotent. But when, by compassion, one experiences a violent sense of the intolerable in the face of the sufferings that torture others, there is no longer room for this sense of impotency.

When, in the mind, we have gained courage, and are willing to take on the suffering of others—once we think of their suffering, we experience a slight discomfort. But once this sense of sadness is past, we are enthusiastic, we feel full of courage, just the opposite of what has occurred before.

We have already spoken of the viewpoint of those who practice the teachings of the Buddha, have we not? The first teaching that they put into practice is discipline, which consists of renouncing the six nonvirtuous acts. The beneficiaries of this practice are animate beings. It is where animate beings are concerned that one forbids oneself to kill, to rob, to abuse sexually, to lie, to slander, to be rough or uncouth. One must begin, then, by no longer doing ill to animate beings, and in this case the object "animate beings" is a necessity: it is in them that discipline finds its support.

The rules of the discipline of individual liberation all consist of renouncing evil done to another, as well as the mental basis of this evil. Once a potential victim appears, one has only to forbid oneself to harm him or her by seeing any harmful act as a great evil. This is how one proceeds in the discipline of individual liberation.

As for the way of the bodhisattvas, generosity, discipline, and patience are necessarily practiced toward animate beings, and patience is the principal practice of the bodhisattvas. Why? Because they must cultivate the spirit of Awakening on the basis of love and compassion. Meditation on love necessarily blocks hate, which is the opposite of love, and patience is necessary since it is the antidote of anger. In order to meditate on patience, then, one needs an object of patience: an enemy.

If we consider things carefully, enemies are essential, almost as essential as spiritual masters. We cannot meditate on patience by taking as our object the Buddha. Patience is addressed only to enemies that agitate your mind, that make you angry. We need them in order to make progress in practice. I shall say nothing, then, of the immense goodness of all beings. It is explained that those whom we regard as enemies, those on whom we turn our backs, those whom we wish to harm are particularly generous with us in this respect.

Likewise, compassion is most essential, and it will have as its object the ensemble of beings afflicted with misery. The way of the Lesser and Greater Vehicles, this marvel, the multiple collections of merits that have been cultivated in them—these practices have as their object living beings, our dear mothers. And these practices that culminate in the authentic and perfect Awakening—in the disappearance of every defect, in the possession of all qualities—these too are reached in taking our brothers and sisters, living beings, as our object.

Shantideva writes in *Journey Toward the Awakening,*

It is through beings, as if through the buddhas,
That one obtains the virtues of a buddha.
Now, the veneration we accord the buddhas,
We deny beings. Why this difference?[3]

To reach the state of the buddha, we must rely simultaneously on ordinary beings and on enlightened beings. It is a very serious error to venerate to the buddhas while neglecting ordinary beings. For that matter, it is in the Buddha that we take refuge, and to him that we devote our faith. Now, the only things that interest this Buddha in whom we have faith are animate beings. Would it not be hypocritical to take refuge in the Buddha while neglecting those to whom the Buddha offers the refuge of his great love? If we truly love the Buddha, it is important that we not do anything that would go contrary to his heart. Is it not lamentable to believe in the Buddha and to mistreat, oppress, despise, and deceive the unfortunate ones that the Buddha only snatches to the "eyelets of his compassion"?

Were it an ordinary being, a really close friend, one would respect his or her sensitivity, one would seek to avoid what displeases that person, one would say to oneself that if one did this, he or she would be sad, that if one ignored that person, he or she would be pained. When one has a friend who is a vegetarian, it is unsuitable to eat meat in his or her presence—this would be to ignore that person. If we are ashamed to take no account of a friend, who is but an ordinary being, then it will be necessary to take a little account of the enlightened opinion of the buddhas and bodhisattvas. This way we have of acting always seems pitiful to me. When one has faith in the Buddha, it is pathetic to regard "ordinary" beings as beings to be crushed, or on whom to "take things out." Those who are Buddhists ought to consider this carefully.

There is no problem for others, if they think that they are at a lecture.

At the moment, I am going to speak as a Buddhist. Having reflected in this way on the spirit of Awakening, Buddhists ought to practice in a spirit of having faith in the Buddha, and loving the Dharma, all the while respecting the enlightened thought of the Buddha.

Even when we are acting only for ourselves, it is in the measure of our altruism that what we do will bring temporary well-being and assistance in the long term. If, on the contrary, we neglect other animate beings through obsession with our own personal good, we fall into the partial vision of nirvana proper to the arhat of the Hearers, which also presents the fault of holding oneself in high esteem. This deficiency is the effect of a lack of esteem for others. Being practitioners, disciples of the Buddha, we shall exercise ourselves in the perfectly pure actions of the Buddha. Of all the Buddha's numerous actions, which counts the most? The spirit of Awakening, which consists of preferring others to oneself.

We shall stick to this direction, then, even if we have not yet attained the goal. The essential is to think that we shall persist even if we have not yet succeeded. As we read in *Journey Toward the Awakening*:

What need of many explanations?
Between the one who acts for himself
And the Buddha who acts for others,
Observe the difference!

Until the present we have, with consciousness and diligence, preferred ourselves to all others. Up until this day, we have done only this: cherish ourselves while disdaining others. And look at the result. Today, now that we have heard some of the defects attached to cherishing oneself, and some of the qualities attached to cherishing others, we ought to concentrate carefully, and to reduce our self-esteem as much as we can, while developing the esteem we have for others to the greatest degree possible. If we do so, the sun of happiness will rise, and the good of others as well as our own personal good will be accomplished. From this moment, we can hope for this. Then tell yourselves this: "I have taken the resolution to exercise myself in the way opened by the bodhisattvas, the children of the Conqueror, by following their perfect example."

What people have the power to accomplish their projects, and to consecrate themselves to the good of others all the way to the accomplishment of their ultimate good? To be capable of doing the good of others with sure foot, using our personal experience, it is indispensable that we have realized what is called the absolute body for oneself. It is necessary to realize the absolute body in order to accomplish the good of others by exchanging the absolute body for the formal body for others. So this is how one must think: "To easily accomplish the ultimate good of all animate beings, my elderly mothers in infinite numbers, I shall myself attain to buddhahood in two bodies."

Here, then, the cause is the aspiration to consecrate oneself to the good of others, and "spirit of Awakening" is the name for the spiritual strength accompanying the aspiration to consecrate oneself to omniscience. At the moment, this is only an artificial idea, and not the authentic spirit of Awakening. We cannot say that we are going to produce the spirit of Awakening today and that we shall instantly be bodhisattvas.

To engender and cultivate the spirit of Awakening, we must meditate on it, meditate again, and always meditate, for a long time, shoring up our meditation with the accumulation of merits and wisdom, and being purified of the veils. If we meditate on this subject without ceasing, then at the end of a great many lives we shall arrive, perhaps. But it may also take kalpas. Nor is it impossible for this to take but a few years.

Be this as it may, and whatever way we have chosen, we shall have to begin by gradually forming a clear idea. Only afterwards shall we move to the experience: at first, experiences with effort, then without effort, and finally without the least artifice, without even having to think about it. Then naturally, spontaneously, the aspiration to consecrate ourselves to the Awakening will splice with the aspiration to consecrate ourselves to the good of others, and, whether we are walking, lying, or sitting, everything will remind us of the spirit of Awakening. Then only shall we have experienced it once and for all. This can only occur at the end of a lengthy training.

THE SEVENFOLD PRAYER

Now that we have well meditated on the spirit of Awakening, and have a clear idea of it, we are going to recite, in order to stabilize this idea, a prayer of aspiration coupled with a ritual. We shall recite the prayer in seven parts in order to accomplish the accumulations and the purification. It is not necessary to recite a particular ritual text.

First, we must evoke the buddhas and bodhisattvas. Next we shall see ourselves surrounded by the unhappy animate beings whose throng reaches to the limits of space. We shall have clearly in mind a compassion and love for beings, and we shall have the faith that is inspired by good. Finally, we shall recall the qualities of body, word, and mind of the buddhas and bodhisattvas. Once you feel inspired, imagine yourselves humbly prostrate before them, rendering them homage with clasped hands.

Next, imagine all possible riches, private goods, and all the pleasant things that belong to no one in particular. Then imagine that you make them an offering to the buddhas and bodhisattvas. But especially see the positive acts that you have accumulated with your body, your word, and your mind as transformed into objects you offer.

Next tell yourself that, although you would not wish to suffer, you have until now accumulated many causes of suffering that have not yet ripened. With the most sincere regret possible, consider that you have ingested a poison, and conceive that you confess this, with a vow never to commit any negative act again.

After this, meditate on the joy, more than on the regret, that the good you have done inspires in you. Then rejoice in all of the positive acts that others have accumulated—in brief, from the benefits accumulated by any ordinary being at all to the positive qualities, the resplendent actions, of the buddhas: rejoice in all of this from the bottom of your heart. You ought to rejoice even in the only kind of good that can be accomplished by poor beginners, appreciating their efforts and not having the least thought of jealousy or rivalry toward them.

We have already spoken of the four bodies of the Buddha, and it is thus that his body of apparition takes on a new existence in terms of those it must convert: it accomplishes the high deed of awakening in the real and perfect Awakening; it turns the wheel of the teachings; and it effects its "passage beyond suffering." In the infinite universes of the worlds, once a body of apparition of the Buddha has accomplished the act of perfect Awakening, it sets the wheel of the Dharma turning. Imagine, then, the buddhas and bodhisattvas who have not yet set the wheel of the teachings turning, and beseech them to deign to teach the Dharma. This is what is called the exhortation to teach.

Next concentrate on those who propose to "pass into nirvana" once they have no more beings to convert under such a form, and implore them not to pass into nirvana.

Finally, think of the six parts of this prayer, from homage to the supplication not to pass into nirvana. All of this will have enabled us to accumulate causes of good. Now none of these causes is destined for an inferior result. May they become the cause by which we shall attain the dignity of the supreme perfect Awakening, for the good of all beings.

It matters little that you cannot pronounce the Tibetan text of this prayer. What is important is to reflect on what it means. We shall read the sheet that has been distributed.

With the thought of liberating all beings, we shall take refuge, declaring that, from now on and to the Awakening, we take refuge in the Buddha, the Dharma, and the Community. As we have seen, there are two manners of taking refuge. The first consists of placing one's hopes in the Three Refuges as different from oneself. The second goes beyond this, since it consists in taking refuge of thinking that one will oneself realize the noble state of the Three Gems. The most important thing is to ask refuge of the buddhas and bodhisattvas who stand before us, in order to be able to realize the Three Refuges ourselves. This, in essence, is how one takes refuge. We must take refuge in the Three Gems resulting from our practice of the way.[4]

When we recite

Practicing love according to knowledge,
I shall strive for the good of beings:
I make before the buddhas
The vow of the spirit of perfect Awakening,

we mean that, putting forth a great effort to practice emptiness with a heart of compassion—that is, love and goodness in the light of transcendent knowledge—we make before the assembly of the buddhas and bodhisattvas the vow to reach buddhahood for the good of all beings.

When we have said, "I shall engender the spirit of Awakening," we shall then have engendered it. I have already explained how one maintains visualization. In pronouncing these words, one will vigorously cultivate this thought, which is the bearer of a double aspiration.

When we have read everything together, we shall conclude with a quatrain drawn from the chapter "Dedication" in *Journey Toward the Awakening*:

So long as space shall last,
May I be found
Where there are beings,
To scatter their suffering![5]

As long as space is not exhausted, and especially as long as that situation lasts in which unfortunate animate beings know not the consolation of well-being, and in which they have neither refuge nor protector, if it is given to me to remain with them—even if I can do nothing great but only as much as I can—I shall toil exclusively to make real what is useful to them. This is the decision to be made.

In reciting the three last lines of this stanza—"May I be found / Where there are beings, / To scatter their suffering!"—we seal, so to speak, the courage that we have already acquired. It is hardly a matter of saying only here, today, before the buddhas and bodhisattvas, that we shall attain of buddhahood for the good of all beings. It is a matter of saying that we shall do absolutely nothing except toil for the good of the other, "so long as space shall last."

As one may read in Nagarjuna's *Jeweled Necklace,* the element of space constitutes the support and terrain in which all animate beings rejoice. Likewise, we ought to have no other thought than that of being the object of rejoicing, the support, and the terrain of all animate beings. We ought to decide that, in life, in death, on the most common occasions as on the ultimate one, we shall no longer do anything else.

At this point, those among you who are to receive the votive spirit of Awakening, and who do not have bad legs, should place their right knee on the ground. If you are hefty, that is a special case. Those who have a massive body, an imposing presence, will remain seated, planted like mountains.

Now relax, and read the text in your language, three times. The master of ceremonies will read the entire prayer once. Then I shall present the text, and it will be read again.

Think that the buddhas and bodhisattvas stand before you. Think that all animate beings surround you. Imagine that the buddhas and bodhisattvas are your witnesses as you make your promise for the good of all beings.

The second repetition is the reformed mind, and after having reflected upon it well, you will make it.

The third and last repetition—here is the state of mind, and the great courage, with which you must proceed to it. You will do everything to keep this excellent and perfect state of mind—the absolute good and pleasing thought of being useful to others— from ever weakening.

Good. Be seated again. Let each of you read the text every day, when there is a bit of time. It is well to reflect on it a little. I too, I think of it all the time. I do not have great experience, but even if one has but a little experience, what good this will do the mind!

They say that in Tibet, the Land of Snows, the whole of the teachings of the two vehicles, as well as that of the tantras, has been preserved. Now, the essential of these teachings can be reduced to the spirit of Awakening. All the teachings of the Lesser Vehicle are the preliminaries to the practice of the spirit of Awakening. The way of the tantras is the action of the spirit of Awakening. The root of all these teachings, then, is this spirit of Awakening. It may be difficult to seize the view of emptiness. It will be easier with the experience of the spirit of Awakening. But if it is easy to understand the notion "spirit of Awakening," it is difficult to have a living experience of it. The spirit of Awakening and the view of emptiness should be the ground of our practice and of our very life. From there on prostrations, circumambulations, purifications, and offerings, which are the deeds of the tantras, will spread out like the branches of the practice of the spirit of Awakening. A number of us neglect the essential to give importance to these secondary practices. This is not correct.

Questions and Answers VII

■ ■ ■ ■

Why is it said that the mind is luminous?

In Tibetan, the word *consciousness* denotes that which knows its object. On what act does the individual rely in order to "know"? On an act of consciousness. The fact of knowing its object is not a conditioned creation of consciousness but its very nature. The clear light, in the expression "innate original clear light," constitutes the basis of the emergence of the way and of fruit. Perhaps it is for this reason that the Buddha has spoken of "clear light." Is this not, in a word, what enables one to eliminate ignorance?

If we do not exist as an independent self, how can we decide anything at all?

As I said this morning, the source of the problem is the inability to distinguish between existing and existing really, not existing and not existing really.

What do you think of euthanasia and abortion?

It is generally better to allow old age and sickness to bring life to an end. To practice euthanasia is to take life. Still, the pros and cons must be weighed in terms of the need of the moment. The same thing for abortion. It is generally reducible to killing. It is better to avoid it. But here too one must weigh the pros and cons.

If we do not have the least attachment, why should we move to act?

We spoke of this this morning. Let us take the example of a consciousness that apprehends flowers. It can apprehend them three ways: one, in the belief that they are real; two, without distinguishing between reality and unreality; and three, judging them unreal. We are not saying that all modes of the apprehension of objects present a defect. Nor is it a defect in the perceptions: to seize good as good and suffering as suffering, here you have something that occurs even at the level of the Buddha. As a consequence, the qualities of the buddhas are expounded as follows: omniscience that knows directly the "how" of things—their essence—and omniscience that knows directly the "how many"— all of their diversity. It is explained that there are one hundred forty-six wisdoms in buddhahood. It is impossible for the Buddha to see nothing or to be able to see nothing.

Can one's spiritual master be a master who is no longer living?

Yes. If he was a master, he continues to be one. If your personal experience and realization never cease to deepen, you will certainly one day encounter the master's body of knowledge.

Is Buddhism a philosophy or a religion?

Both. Some call it a science of the mind or spirit.

Do you think that the science of psychology can serve as a support for the practice of Buddhism in the West?

There are convergences and divergences. I think that, generally speaking, Western psychology has as its object only the mental activities of this life. It explains only this life and never speaks of habits inherited from previous lives. This is radically different from Buddhism. Psychology seeks explanation solely on the basis of the fluctuations of the body. It sometimes has many difficulties when it finds no explanation. When psychology explains the emergence of the various contents of thought, it is in terms of the experiences of this life alone. Or again, it imagines that it is possible to explain everything from a point of departure in physical behavior. But psychology does not succeed in giving a good explanation of what it thinks it is naturally able to explain.

A number of states of mind, according to the Buddhist explanation, present themselves when old propensities acquired in former lives are reawakened. The origin of these states of mind is not limited to the present life, since they are the reawakening of earlier habits. I find it difficult, using only the external and internal circumstances of this life, to explain these mental states. Parapsychologists should take this opinion into serious consideration.

We generally find that science has limits. Can all phenomena be explained within the confines of these limits? The question seems difficult to me. Phenomena do not all occur within the confines of these limits. Up until now, then, science has restricted itself to a limited endeavor consisting essentially of calculations and measurements. When, little by little, science has expanded, I think that its object will expand as well.

Jesus lived after the Buddha. Can we see in him a manifestation of the primordial Buddha?

Here is how Buddhists see the matter. The teachers of this world, holy beings useful to those they seek to help, are primary and secondary manifestations of the buddhas and bodhisattvas. One can say this. I would add: One *must* say this.

Are our decisions and choices products of karma?

We hear of "actions analogous to their causes." We briefly touched on the subject this morning. If in our preceding life we have contracted the habit of killing, then in our succeeding reincarnation we naturally have a tendency to commit acts analogous to their cause, here, to kill insects and other animate beings. The decision to kill is undoubtedly the effect of a habit acquired in the preceding life. I could not say whether, generally speaking, the negative emotions proceed from karma. We have spoken of this, but I should not be able to say whether this decision, too, is subject to karma.

What should one think of the insanity of those who have lost the sense of analysis?

If you are asking me why people become insane, you are seeking a medical opinion. I prefer to speak of karma. The general explanation is that there are causes and conditions. We must distinguish between principal causes and secondary causes, or temporary conditions. In the area of causes, then, karma is the most powerful element. As for conditions, there are three types, themselves conditioned by various sudden changes. But in the last analysis, the emergence of conditions obeys karma. Still, whatever the karma of the moment—and it can be positive or negative—this is the karma that the conditions will obey.

Concluding Words

■ ■ ■ ■

I thank you. I am very happy that this third opportunity to tie a spiritual knot with one another, thanks to this meeting in France, has been pleasant and successful. I should like to thank you for this. I should like to say to all of you, as we have already said, that it is important for each of us to attend to our mind. If you have a religion, practice it well. Examine things well, and if you act against your religion, observe your mind, and with memory, vigilance, and attention try to stop. Force yourself to hold back. I think self-discipline is primary and fundamental.

If you have no religion, watch yourself closely. When you see that you are going to harm another, restrain yourself. If you succeed in being useful to others in your life, the aim of our meeting will have been attained.

I have not come here for fun, or to tell stories. I seek happiness of mind. You seek happiness of mind as well. Then what have we done? We have met together to reflect on the way to know happiness of mind.

Well, now I say good-bye to you. I think we shall meet again soon. In any case, whether we see each other again or not, we must lead constructive lives. We must have compassion. Life should not be destructive. That is the essential thing.

Endnotes

■ ■ ■ ■

INTRODUCTION: LAYING THE GROUNDWORK

1. The gods (Sanskrit, *deva;* Tibetan, *lha*) make up one of the five or six spheres of existence of samsara, the cycle of birth and rebirth. The world of the gods is a sphere of appearance dominated and conditioned by the spiritual poison of pride. The dragons (*naga, klu*) resemble serpents and belong to the sphere of the animals; they rule over the element water and the riches stored underground. The perfume-eaters (*gandharva, driza*) are the celestial musicians of the world of desire.

2. The three worlds (*triloka; khams-gsum*) are the whole of samsara, from the most gross to the most subtle: the world of desire, the world of form, and the world of the formless. The six classes of beings (*shadgat; 'gro-drug*) that are prisoners of samsara are divided into higher rebirths (gods, demigods, and human beings) and lower rebirths (beasts, pretas or frustrated spirits, and infernal worlds). See Patrul Rinpoche, *The Words of My Perfect Teacher,* trans. Padmakara Translation Group (San Francisco: HarperCollins, 1994), pt.1, ch. 3. The four births (*caturyoni; skye-gnas bzhi*) are the ways that beings provided with a "body" can be born: of a womb, such as human beings; of an egg, such as birds; by miracle, as the gods; or of moisture, as certain insects.

3. Actually, at Sarnath, in northern India.

4. *Pancabhadraparishadya; 'khor lnga-sde bzang-po*: The five companions of Siddhartha Gautama; they were the first whom the Buddha instructed and ordained as monks.

5. The second of the five gradual ways of the total Awakening according to the Greater Vehicle. This is the final preparation for the way called "of vision," in which general insubstantiality is perceived in all its brilliance.

6. *Vajropamasamadhi; rdo-rje lta-bu'i ting-nge-'dzin*: Indestructible and irresistible as diamond, this recollection marks the definitive end of all veils and impurities; and, as a "way on which nothing any longer constitutes an obstacle" (*bar-chad med lam*) it opens out upon the Awakening of the Lesser or Greater Vehicle, depending on the view of the practitioner.

7. *Nirmanakaya; sprul-sku*: A manifestation of the Awakening destined to convert the beings whose karma is still impure. This body is called supreme when it designates a being such as the Buddha or the incarnation of a totally accomplished master.

8. This nonexistence defines what is called insubstantiality or gross vacuity.

9. *Nairatmya; bdag-med*: *Substance* denotes what is in itself and by itself. That is *substantial* which, being its own cause, subsists independently of anything else. The word *insubstantiality*, then, denotes the essence of all that is not substance in the strictly philosophical sense.

10. *Dashabhumi; sa-bcu*: The spiritual levels traversed by the bodhisattvas on the ways of vision and meditation as they journey to the authentic and perfect Awakening.

11. The methods are the virtues themselves, and knowledge designates the purity, or emptiness, of the subject, the object, and the beneficiary of each positive act.

12. Depth designates emptiness and vastness, the methods of Awakening adapted to each subject.

13. The Buddha pronounced three cycles of teaching—Four Noble Truths, emptiness, and the clear light—and the tantras.

14. The *prajnaparamita* (*shes-rab-kyi pha-rol-tu phyin-pa*) is the direct knowledge, or "realization," of emptiness.

15. Asanga's *Mahayana-Uttaratantra-shastra,* also translated "Unsurpassable Continuum."

16. *Tathagatagarbha-sutra.*

17. *Prabhasvara; 'od-gsal*: "Brightness" or "luminosity," appears in all three cycles but is exhaustively expounded only in the third. The Lesser Vehicle knows of it, as shown in this passage from the *Anguttarakaya,* I: "The clear light is the mind that can sometimes be blemished by negative emotions, but that otherwise is free of them." See Lamotte, *L'Enseignement de Vimalakirti* ("Vimalakirti's teaching"), Bibliotheque du Muséon (Louvain, 1962), 51:52. At the level of the Greater Vehicle of the Transcendences, this decla-

ration appears at the beginning of the *Sutra of Transcendent Knowledge in Eight Thousand Stanzas*: "The mind? The mind does not really exist. The essence of the mind is the clear light."

18. Or transcendent knowledge under its primordial aspect, as described in the sutras of the third cycle, such as the *Sutra of the Entry into Lanka (Lankavatarasutra)*: the very substance of the qualities of the absolute body of the Awakening; the non-nothingness of clear vacuity.

19. *Shakyasingha; Shakya Seng-ge:* A name of the Buddha, whose teachings, compared to the lion's roar, "terrify the hideous heretical beasts."

20. In Tibetan, *bskal-pa:* era, cosmic period. A great kalpa corresponds to the cycle of the formation, duration, and disappearance of the universe. Great kalpas beyond measure designate 10^{59} great kalpas.

21. *Pitaka; sde-snod.* We would say "literature."

22. Whereas the Vehicle of the Transcendences and the lower vehicles are "causal," the Diamond Vehicle is "resultant," since its practice is the actual activity of buddhahood rather than anything leading to it.

23. *Guhyamantra-vajrayana; gsang-sngags rdo-rje'i thegpa.*

24. One who has reached the real nature, another name of the Buddha.

25. Here, and in the rest of the text, *mode* is most often a synonym for "manner of being" or "of existing."

26. *Tathata; de-bzhin-nyid:* The simplicity of the real in all its evidence.

27. The literal sense of the Tibetan *drang-don,* where *drang* is the future of *'dren,* "to guide."

28. True for the Buddhists, but not necessarily for others.

29. The very sense of "vast."

30. During the "yoga of the body" of the phase of creation.

31. In brief, one envisions the body of a man or woman who inspires desire and attachment as a bag stuffed with innards and repugnant things.

32. What ethic it inspires, as it were.

33. *Tirthikas; mu-steg-pa:* Philosophers and mystics who believe in eternal being or in nothingness.

34. The five sensory organs that we know, plus the "mental" organ (*manas; yid*). Every sensory perception results from the coincidence of three phenomena: the object of a given sense, the organ corresponding to it, and consciousness, which clarifies the perception and makes it known.

35. Visual, auditory, olfactory, gustatory, tactile, and mental.

36. As Heidegger, for example, wondered: "What actually is the being of a being?"

37. *Satyadvaya-vibhaga:* Literally, "distinction of the two truths."

38. *Abhisamayalankara; mNgon-rtogs rgyan.*
39. *Mula-madhyamaka-vritti. Prasannapada:* Commentary on Nagarjuna's *Fundamental Treatise.*

QUESTIONS AND ANSWERS I

1. The external aspect of the master matters little. His words count far more: not the words he pronounces but their meaning; not their provisional meaning but their ultimate signification. And to listen to him well will be the deed no longer of dualistic consciousness but of omniscience and nondiscursive wisdom.
2. The collection of sutras, scholastic texts (*abhidharma*), and disciplinary regulations (*vinaya*).
3. *Tarkajvala:* A commentary on his *Quintessence of the Middle Way* (*Madhyamaka-hridaya*).
4. *Moksha; thar-pa:* Liberation from the suffering caused by primordial ignorance.
5. The "void" in its metaphysical and mystical sense.

THE SELF AND KARMA

1. Nonviolence (*ahimsa; mi-'tshe-ba*) is practiced by vegetarianism and so on. Interdependent production (*pratityasamutpada; rten-'byung*) is another name for vacuity.
2. *Manovijnana.*
3. *Alayavijnana.*
4. *Klishta-manovijnana.*
5. In Tibetan, *tshogs-brgyad:* The five sensory consciousnesses, plus mental consciousness, mental consciousness sullied by negative emotions, and fundamental consciousness.
6. *Vajravali.*
7. In Tibetan, *gSang-ba 'dus-pa:* One of the "father" tantras of the Unsurpassable Tantras.
8. *Pudgala:* Synonym for "self."
9. See page 132 n. 12, on the sevenfold reasoning.
10. *Upadana, nye-bar len-pa:* Element of interdependent production perpetuating our psychic continuum in an uninterrupted way and constraining us to believe that this element is best for us.
11. Note, for example, the power of the designation "the year 2000." Although

it is completely relative, it stirs a millenarian emotion in the great majority of people.

12. Literally, "Tantras of the Unsurpassable Yoga," *Anuttara-yoga-tantra* (*bla-na med-pa'i rnal-'byor-gyi rgud*). The tantras are practiced in the following stages: (1) *kriya*, in which the emphasis falls on the ritual activities; (2) *carya*, in which these activities are combined with the natural state of deity; (3) *yoga*, in which this natural state is shared with the deity; and (4) *anuttara* ("unsurpassable"), in which the natural state of the deity and that of the adept have never been distinct things. The *anuttara* is divided into father, mother, and neither father nor mother, that is, into *maha*, where the emphasis falls on the phase of creation; *anu*, where it falls on the phase of perfection; and *atti*, or Great Perfection (*rdzogs-pa chen-po*).

13. See Lati Rinpoché and J. Hopkins, *La Mort, l'Etat Intermédiaire et la Renaissance dans le Bouddhisme Tibétain* ("Death, the intermediate state, and rebirth, in Tibetan Buddhism"), (Editions Dharma, 1980), pp. 44–46. Patrul Rinpoche, *The Words of My Perfect Teacher*.

14. *Vasana; bag-chags.*

15. In Tibetan, *gsal-tsam rig-tsam.*

16. It constitutes the object of distinction in samsara and nirvana.

17. In Tibetan, *gsog-pa: Register,* rather than the usual *accumulate,* since there are acts that are executed but not registered (*byas-la ma-bsags-pa*), which will have no succeeding effect.

18. Vasubandhu's *Abhidharmakosha.*

19. Chandrakirti's *Madhyamakavatara*—the threshold, as it were, of Magarjuna's *Fundamental Treatise.*

20. In Tibetan, *nam mkha'i rdul.* See below.

21. A universe cannot arise spontaneously. Its cause is to be sought in the preceding universe.

22. Or the real (*dharmata; chos-nyid*).

23. *Shunyata-saptati-karika.*

24. Of interdependent production: ignorance, karmic composition, consciousness, name and form, sources of perception, contact, sensations, thirst, appropriation, becoming, birth, old age and death.

25. Lalande, in his philosophical dictionary, explains that naive realism is "a belief of common sense, which uncritically accepts the existence of a world of material objects and conscious subjects, with which consciousness is in an ill-defined relationship, conceived either as the direct apprehension of things or beings different from the subject, or as a relationship analogous to that of a portrait and its model."

QUESTIONS AND ANSWERS II

1. One of the four great schools of practice of Tibetan Buddhism.
2. The two *universal* criteria of true cognition are direct sensory perception and deductive reasoning.
3. Practice begins with intellectual comprehension (*go-ba*), deepens in the meditative experience (*nyams-myong*) of happiness, clarity, and/or non-thought, is stabilized in realization (*rtogs-pa*), and culminates in liberation (*grol-ba*).
4. *Santana; rgyud:* Mind and body are made up of material particles and instants of consciousness, whose combination and uninterrupted succession form a package that, like a river, seems to constitute a unity, and that we believe real, or substantial, as they present themselves to gross observation.
5. *Abhisheka; dbang-bskur,* which reveals the perfection of our bodies, word, mind, qualities, and activities. The "manifestations of wisdom," then, designate all possible experiences and realizations.
6. The Buddha's personal name was Gautama Siddhartha.
7. *Dharma; chos* denotes both teachings and realities or phenomena.
8. Extremist; this is the desire for the absolute or nothingness.
9. His Holiness here employs the English expression "individual identity."
10. Literally, maturation (*vipaka; rnam-smin*).
11. *bLo-sbyong:* Practices of exchange, equality, and so on.
12. *Bodhicaryavatara; Byang-chub sems-dpa'i spyod-pa-la 'jug-pa:* The major work of Shantideva and the greatest Madhyamika-Prasangika poem.
13. *Shamatha:* "Mental calm," the practice of concentration.
14. Confession rests on four forces: support, regret, resolution, and conduct.

SUFFERING AND THE ORIGIN OF SUFFERING

1. Another possible translation of *vasana; bag-chags:* "habitual schemata."
2. For the essential difference between the philosophical "I" and the sense of the "I," or "innate self," see *Comprendre la vacuité* ("Understanding vacuity") (Padmakara, 1993), pp. 44–55, 163–76.
3. See Patrul Rinpoche, *The Words of My Perfect Teacher;* Lati Rinpoché and É. Hopkins, *Mort dans le Bouddhisme Tibetain,* "Les tapes de la Mort' ("Stages of death"), pp. 33–34; as well as the various translations of the *Book of the Dead* (Tib., *Bar-do thos-grol*).
4. In other words, appearance, growth, near obtaining, and clear light, experi-

ences described in Lati Rinpoché and Hopkins, *Mort dans le Bouddhisme Tibetain*, pp. 43–54; and under the nouns "Clarté" ("brilliance"), "Croissance" ("growth"), "Obtention" ("obtaining"), and "Claire Lumière de l'Instant Fondamental" ("clear light of the fundamental instant") in Patrul Rinpoche, *The Words of My Pefect Teacher*.

5. One of His Holiness's tutors.

6. Seat of the Tibetan government in exile, in northern India.

7. The body and the consciousness bound to the body.

8. The latter has two effects conforming to their cause, one active and the other passive. See Patrul Rinpoche, *The Words of My Perfect Teacher*, pp. 157–58.

9. Asanga's *Abhidharma-samuccaya*.

10. Three of the six teachings of Naropa. The other three are interior warmth, the illusory body, and the transfer of consciousness. See Chögyam Trungpa, *Jeu d'Illusion, Vie et Enseignement de Naropa* ("Play of illusion: Nairpoa's life and teaching"), Points-Sagesse (Paris: Seuil), 1997.

11. *Ayushman-Nanda-Garbhavakranti-nirdesha*.

12. *Prajna-nama Mulamadhyamikakakâ* bk 18, ch. 5.

13. "*Karma-klesha-kshayan mokshas karma-klesha vikalpatah te prapancat . . .*"

14. "*. . . prapancas tu shunyatayam nirudhyate.*"

15. *Shunyatayam:* Locative case of *shunyata.*

16. Or substantialism, which accords absolute being to certain objects.

17. See Jeffrey Hopkins, *Meditation on Emptiness* (London: Wisdom, 1983), pp. 96–97.

QUESTIONS AND ANSWERS III

1. If things are [inter]dependent, they do not exist "in themselves," and so are empty.

2. As in a certain Western-style Buddhism. We might note that a majority of believers on this planet accept reincarnation of the same individual.

3. Since it shows the real essence of the object analyzed.

4. Not only visual, of course. In Tibetan, and basically, "appearance" (*snang-ba*) is a synonym for "perception," "perceived object."

5. *Vastusamgraha:* In Tibetan, *gZhi bsdu ba.*

6. *Bhumivastu,* also called *Bodhisattvabhumi.*

7. If it really existed, it would be immovable, but no phenomenon has ever been seen that never changes.

8. *Prajnaparamita-hridaya,* known in the West as the *Heart Sutra.*

9. The aggregate of "form" here denotes matter, and not only the objects of sight. The other four aggregates are empty as well.

10. Since suffering is "retribution" for negative acts, its experience exhausts these acts.

11. Interchanging oneself and the other. See Dilgo Khyentsé, *Audace et Compassion* ("Daring and compassion"), (Padmakara, 1993), pp. 31–32. Chögyam Trungpa, *L'Entraînement de l'Esprit et l'Apprentissage de la Bienveillance* ("The training of the mind and the apprenticeship of benevolence"), Points-Sagesse (Paris: Seuil), 1998.

12. By the practice of *tonglen* (literally, "giving and taking"): giving one's happiness to others and taking upon oneself all their misfortunes. See Dilgo Khyentsé, *Audace et Compassion,* pp. 38–39.

13. Bk. 5, ch. 13.

14. *Journey Toward the Awakening,* bk. 5, ch. 12.

THE BODIES OF THE BUDDHA, TRAINING, AND SPIRITUAL MASTERS

1. *Nges-pa lnga:* The five certitudes of the body of enjoyment are (1) the place, which is the loftiest pure field; (2) the body, provided with thirty-two major marks and eighty minor marks; (3) temporal certitude: the body of enjoyment will last as long as there are beings to save; (4) his teaching is surely the Greater Vehicle; and (5) his entourage, or audience, is necessarily constituted of sublime bodhisattvas.

2. *Bhadrakalpa, bskal-pa bzang-po.*

3. The Three Roots are the spiritual masters, roots of blessings; the yidam deities, roots of accomplishments; and the dakinis, roots of activities and supreme felicity.

4. The *takloung* school, of the valley of the Tigris, north of Lhasa, is a kagyu tradition emanating from Takloung Thangpa Trashi Pal, the most devoted disciple of Phagmo Droupa. In 1276 Sangye Ön, disciple of Takloung Thangpa, founded at Kham the great monastery of Riwoche. Shapdroung Rinpoche, who recently died, was an eminent representative of this tradition.

5. Dilgo Khyentsé Rinpoche (1910–1990), incarnation of Jamyang Khyentse Wangpo, a great promoter of ecumenism, or knowledge of all the traditions of Tibetan Buddhism. Khyentse Rinpoche was one of the masters of His

Holiness and numerous other lamas. Revealer of Treasures (*termas*) and wise, enlightened poet of our era, he studied with 120 masters. He spent twenty years in meditation in the high Tibetan solitudes and consecrated the rest of his life to continuous teaching, including in the West.

6. See Gampopa, *Ornament of Liberation,* ch. 2.

7. Of Hearers, eremitic buddhas, and the Greater Vehicle.

8. In this they are only appreciating the central thesis of certain sutras of the Greater Vehicle, such as the *Saddharmapundarika*. See *Le Sûtra du Lotus* ("The Sutra of the Lotus") (Paris: Fayard, 1997): "L'espace intérieur" ("The inner space").

9. *Catuhshataka-shastra-karika,* which describes the yogas of the bodhisattva.

10. Among the beasts and pretas (frustrated spirits), and in the underworld.

11. *Bodhipathapradipa.*

12. In Tibetan, *don spyod pa* and *don mthun pa.*

13. By Ashvaghosha, author of the *Buddhacaritas* and contemporary of Nagarjuna.

14. *Guruyoga; bla ma'i rnal 'byor.*

15. See Patrul Rinpoche, *The Words of My Perfect Teacher,* pt.1, ch. 4. It is a matter of the fourth series of meditations, whose object is "to turn the mind from samsara" (*blo-ldog rnam-bzhi*).

16. See Patrul Rinpoche, *The Words of My Perfect Teacher,* pt.1, ch.3.

17. See Patrul Rinpoche, *The Words of My Perfect Teacher,* pp. 53–54.

18. See Patrul Rinpoche, *The Words of My Perfect Teacher,* pp. 33–34.

QUESTIONS AND ANSWERS IV

1. Or its expulsion. See Patrul Rinpoche, *The Words of My Perfect Teacher,* pt. 3, ch.1.

2. *Kun-tu bZang-po:* "Perfection Forever," which reveals the primordial purity of all phenomena.

3. His Holiness uses the English expression "self-creation."

4. In Tibetan, *Lhan cig dmigs nges.*

5. The eighty principal physical qualities of the Great Being, to which are added thirty-two "minor" marks.

6. *Sgrol-ma:* The "Liberator," a female buddha, so named because of her promptness in saving beings from all fears. Tradition ascribes to her twenty-one aspects—according to her activities, her color, her attributes, and so on. A book in French is devoted to her: Bokar Rimpotché, *Tara, le Divin au Féminin* ("Tara, the Divine in the feminine"), (Vernègues [13]: Claire Lumière), 1997.

7. When she made her vow to attain omniscient buddhahood for the good of all beings.

REFUTATION OF THE SELF

1. The Nirgranthas, disciples of Parshva, who accepted karmic causality and who are not to be confused with the Jains Clothed in Space (Digambaras).
2. *Shamatha.*
3. *Vipashyana.*
4. More precisely, "attention-memory" (*smriti, dran-pa*).
5. *Pratimoksha; so-thar,* followed by the adepts of the Lesser Vehicle.
6. *Prashrabdhi; shin tu sbyangs pa:* Peace and lightness of body and mind, dissolving all resistance to the accomplishment of good.
7. A generic expression denoting the world of desire, or first level; the world of form, which is divided into four levels, from the first to the fourth *dhyan*; and the formless world, which is divided into four levels, namely, infinite space, infinite consciousness, nothingness, and the sphere neither conscious nor unconscious, also called the summit of becoming.
8. In Tibetan, *nyer bsdogs mi lcog med.* The four concentrations are in turn divided into nine levels (Tib., *bsam gtan sa dgu*): (1) preparation for the first concentration, where there is nothing that cannot be done; (2) simple first concentration; (3) special first concentration; (4) preparation for the second concentration; (5) second concentration; (6) preparation for the third concentration; (7) third concentration; (8) preparation for the fourth concentration; (9) fourth concentration.
9. In this preparatory concentration, it is possible to repel all the gross negative emotions of the world of desire, to attain to the world of form, and then to attain to the formless world, which constitutes the "higher worlds."
10. *Yid la byed pa drug:* The six forms of attention. The mental factor of attention, or mental engagement, designates the mind firmly concentrated on its object. The six forms of attention are (1) attention to a correct understanding of the character of the higher and lower worlds; (2) attention to an appreciation of the qualities of the higher worlds, which deepens the preceding attention in the quietude of higher vision; (3) attention to a rejection of the negative emotions, which permits the elimination of the most manifest degrees of the negative emotions of the world of desire; (4) attention to the accumulation of joy, which, enlightened by a felicity of a lower type, dissolves the negative emotions of the world of desire of an intermediate level; (5) attention entirely devoted to an examination of the

mind, in order to trace the subtle negative emotions, and in doing so to eliminate them; (6) attention to the countermeasures: application of the antidotes.

11. In this fashion a distinction is drawn between concentration as cause (its actual practice) and concentration as effect, which is one of the four formless spheres.

12. See n. 7.

13. Which His Holiness does not name, and which represent the aggregates and all of the categories of scholasticism developed in the literature of the *Abhidharma*.

14. That is, thusness (*tathata*), or vacuity, which impregnates all phenomena.

15. Literally, "in diamond or in half diamond," that is, with the legs crossed and both feet tucked under the opposite knee.

16. Or *Atiyoga*, "Great Perfection," the loftiest vehicle of the Awakening in the Nyingmapa system.

17. *rLung-ro*, or "residual breaths."

18. In Tibetan, *rtsa-gsum 'khor-lo lnga:* The three lateral channels and the five chakras.

19. Six "forces" intervene, which will aid the mind to pose itself. They are (1) study, or hearing, which permits the posing of the mind; (2) reflection, for posing it lastingly; (3) attention-memory, for re-posing it and laying it to rest perfectly; (4) watchfulness, for subduing and pacifying it; (5) courage, for pacifying it perfectly and concentrating it on a single point; and (6) familiarity, for leaving it at one with itself all the way to the state called in Tibetan *mnyam-bzhag*. The first two stations of the mind constitute a forced process; stations three to seven, an interrupted process; the eighth, an uninterrupted process; and the last, the state of profound recollection.

20. In Tibetan, *gnas-ngan-len*, the contrary of suppleness (*shin-sbyangs*).

21. In Tibetan, *ting-nge-'dzin*, profound recollection of mind.

22. In Tibetan, *mtshan-bcas-kyi rnal-'byor*. In meditating, one visualizes oneself as one's tutelary deity but does not regard oneself as its equal in wisdom: the absolute is still an ideal to be attained.

23. In Tibetan, *mtshan-med-kyi rnal-'byor*: Meditation on the spirit of absolute Awakening, emptiness, as a state into which adepts enter, in which they abide, and from which they emerge.

24. In Tibetan, *bskyed-rim*. In order to dissolve the karmic imprints left by the four types of birth, practitioners train themselves to recognize in their ordinary body, word, and mind the awakened body, word, and mind of their tutelary deities.

25. An understanding of the Madhyamika-Prasangika philosophy.
26. That is, until one perceives it as a dream.
27. Then why perpetuate suffering?

QUESTIONS AND ANSWERS V

1. Asanga's *Madhyantavibhaga*.
2. In Tibetan, *rdzogs-rim*: Special practices of transcendent knowledge permitting the actualization of the clear light through the experiences of the four void consciousnesses (see above), once the quintessential channels, breaths, and drops are sufficiently pure in the practitioner's adamantine body. This experience of the clear light is inseparable from the innate wisdom induced by the four joys associated with inner warmth.
3. Great Nyingmapa master (1308–1363), prolific writer on the universality of the Great Perfection (*Atiyoga*), whose life can be read in French in Longchenpa, *La Liberté Naturelle de l'Esprit* ("The natural freedom of the mind") (in Tibetan, *Rang-grol skor-gsum*), Points-Sagesse (Paris: Seuil), 1994, pp. 57–68. *The Treasure of the Magic Gem* (Tib., *Yid-bzhin rin-po-che'i mdzod*) is one of the "Seven Treasures" or perfect treatises revealing the omnipresence of Great Perfection in all the teachings of the Buddha.
4. *Kalacakra-Tantra; Dus-kyi 'khor-lo:* insurpassable Tantra, so named because it places its exterior phase, its interior phase, and its "other" phase in relationship with all possible systems entailing basis, way, and fruit.
5. Great Nyingmapa scholar and master (1846–1912) who devoted himself with the same genius to the "vulgar" arts of grammar, logic, medicine, astrology, and so on as to the mystical sciences of the mind (writing commentaries on an ocean of sutras and tantras), to the heights of the poetry of the Awakening, to the most arduous treatises, to the methods of accomplishment of the deities (*sadhanas*), and to ritual. His works fill thirty two volumes.
6. Or karmic formations (Tib., *'du-byed*). I have chosen the word *compositions* to show that this psychic aggregate is the machine producing the concepts and behaviors associated with composed phenomena (Tib., *'dus-byas*).

THE PATH TO ULTIMATE OMNISCIENCE

1. The vanquisher of ignorance and suffering is the Buddha.
2. A thing can arise from (1) itself, (2) another thing, (3) itself and another thing, or (4) neither itself nor another thing.

3. No "judgment of reality" has ever been able definitively to embrace the real.
4. *Ratnavali:* Counsels of Nagarjuna to his friend King Udayana of Vatsa.
5. His or her body and all the states of his or her mind.
6. Bk. 9, ch. 25.
7. Independent of any knowledge or idea that thinking beings can have of it.
8. Such as anger, inebriation, and so on.
9. As if it were, for example, an integral part of Matthew's physical appearance.
10. And it is thus that their philosophy is the most suitable for an understanding and explanation of the extraordinary practices of the Vehicle of the Tantras.
11. "Primordial matter" (*gtso-bo*), or "nature" (*prakriti rang-bzhin*), is made up of three qualities (*guna*), whose combination forms all objects: thus it is cause and effect, both at the same time. See Khenchen Kunzang Palden, "L'Ambroisie des paroles de Manjushri" ("Ambrosia of the words of Manjushri"), in his *Comprendre la Vacuité,* pp. 81–84.
12. "I" do not really exist because (1) I am not my aggregates (my body and my mind); (2) I am not anything besides my aggregates; (3) I am not the foundation of my aggregates; (4) I do not have my aggregates as a real foundation; (5) I am not the real proprietor of my aggregates; (6) I am not the simple ensemble of my aggregates; and (7) I am not the form of my aggregates. See Hopkins, *Meditation on Emptiness,* p. 48.

QUESTIONS AND ANSWERS VI

1. The Tibetan *gdung-ma* literally means "beam" or "girder," and here denotes the starting point of the way.

PRACTICING THE TEACHINGS

1. The spirit of Awakening is votive as long as the wish to attain to omniscience for the good of all beings remains. It is active when the bodhisattva practices the transcendent virtues. The vow of the active spirit of Awakening, then, is the promise to practice the transcendent virtues with the aim of attaining omniscience.
2. Bk. 8, chs. 95–96.
3. Bk. 6, ch. 113.
4. Literally, in the "refuge-fruit."
5. Bk. 10, ch. 55.

Glossary

■ ■ ■ ■

Aggregates, five (Sanskrit, *pancaskandha*; Tibetan, *phung-po lnga*): The individual's body and mind: forms (or matter), sensations, perceptions, the karmic compositions, and the consciousnesses.

Aids of the Awakening (*bodhipaksha; byang-phyogs so-bdun*): The four fixations of attention, the four authentic eliminations, the four bases of the miraculous powers, the five pure faculties, the seven branches of the Awakening, and the eight-fold path.

Arhat (Tib., *dgra-bcom-pa*): Being who has attained liberation at the conclusion of the way of the Lesser Vehicle.

Aryadeva (Tib., *'Phags-pa Lha*): The most celebrated disciple of Nagarjuna, on whose thought he wrote commentaries in several treatises in which Chandrakirti was to recognize the authentic intention of the master preserved in the Prasangika tradition. He lived in the third century.

Asanga (Tib., *Thogs-med*): One of the Six Ornaments of the World, who lived in the fourth century. Accomplished devotee of Maitreya, who instructed him on the progressive realization of the hidden meaning of the sutras of the Greater Vehicle, which Asanga transcribed in his five celebrated treatises (*Byams-chod sde-inga*). He is regarded as the founder of the Chittamatra school.

Atisha Dipamkara: Great Indian master and scholar (982–1054) who taught at the Buddhist university of Vikramashila. An adept of the monastic life, he traveled as far as Indonesia, receiving from Suvarnadvipa the teachings on the spirit of Awakening (*bodhicitta*). He spent the last twelve years of his life in Tibet, teaching and translating. His Tibetan disciples founded the Kadampa school.

Awakening (*bodhi; byang-chub*): The end of all emotional and cognitive impurities, and the realization of all the qualities.

Bardo (*antarabhava; bar-do*): Intermediate state of death, of becoming, of a dream, et cetera.

Bhavaviveka (Tib., *Legs-idan-'byed*): Indian master, author of the *Gleaming Necklace of Transcendent Knowledge*, in which he expounds the arguments of the Madhyamika–Svatantrika school, whose founder he is reputed to be.

Bodhisattva (Tib., *byang-chub sems-dpa'*): A mystic who, having pronounced the vow of the spirit of Supreme Awakening, is an adept of emptiness with a heart of compassion.

Buddhapalita (Tib., *Sangs-rgyas-bskyangs*): Indian master of Madhyamika. Buddhapalita wrote a great commentary on Nagarjuna's *Fundamental Treatise*, all of whose arguments he systematized, thereby becoming the ancestor of the Prasangika school, whose philosophy is the subtlest and loftiest of the four schools of Buddhist thought.

Chandrakirti (Tib., *Zla-ba grags-pa*): A great Madhyamika of the seventh century. Abbot or rector of the university of Nalanda, Chandrakirti committed himself to elucidate both the language and the meaning of the Middle Way. Taking up the ideas of Buddhapalita, Chandrakirti is, properly speaking, the founder of the Madhyamika–Prasangika school. His *Introduction to the Middle Way* (*Madhyamakavatara*) shows the perfect harmony between the teachings on emptiness and the teachings on the clear light.

Chittamatrin (Tib., *sems-tsam-pa*): Philosophical school of the

Greater Vehicle for which the mind really exists, but its objects are only dreams.

Dharma: Generally, the teachings of the Buddha, but also, in the expression "the Dharmas," phenomena, realities.

Dharmakirti (Tib., *Chos-grags*): One of the Six Ornaments of the World, who lived in the sixth century. Native of the South of India (Kanci), instructed by Ishvarasena, a disciple of Dingnaga, he wrote abundant commentaries on Dingnaga's works.

Dingnaga (Tib., *Phyogs-kyi gLang-po*): One of the Six Ornaments of the World, who lived before the sixth century. He incarnates the perfection of logic and gnoseology (*tshad-ma rig-pa*). Son of a rajah, he studied with Vasubandhu. He is the founder of the Buddhist gnoseological tradition.

Eremitic buddha (*pratyekabuddha; rang-sangs-rgas*): A mystic who practices in solitude, without a master and without anyone's knowledge.

Hearer (*shravaka; nyan-thos*): Properly, a direct disciple of the Buddha. Otherwise, a mystic who, having heard the instructions of a master, puts them into practice and makes them heard by others.

Interdependent production (*pratityasamutpada; rten-'brel*): Composed of twelve elements (Tib., *rten-'brel*)—ignorance, karmic composition, consciousness, name and form, sources of perception, contact, sensations, thirst, appropriation, becoming, birth, old age and death.

Jnanagarbha (Tib., *Ye-shes snying-po*): Indian Madhyamika-Svatantrika master of the seventh to the eighth century.

Karma (*las*): Not causality, which arises from the nature of things, but its effect with respect to the mind. Karma is related to the intention underlying the act. The good act brings happiness; the bad act, suffering.

Madhyamika (Tib., *dbU-ma-pa*): The Middle Way, a school of the Greater Vehicle that accepts the union of the two fundamental truths beyond the extremes of eternalism and nihilism.

Maitreya (Tib., *Byams-pa*): Bodhisattva incarnating love and benevolence. Residing for the moment in the heavens of Tushita, whence he is to descend to succeed Shakyamuni, becoming the fifth buddha of the Good Age.

Manjughosha (Tib., *'Jam-pa'i db Yangs*) or Manjushri (*'Jam-pa'i dPal*): This bodhisattva personifies transcendent knowledge. He and Maitreya are among the eight great bodhisattvas who sit at the feet of the Buddha Shakyamuni.

Middle Way: See Madhyamika.

Nagarjuna (Tib., *kLu-sgrub*): One of the Six Ornaments of the World. In tradition, the great master was born into a family of Brahmans of the South of India four hundred years after the *parinirvana* of the Buddha Shakyamuni. While still an adolescent, he attained to perfect knowledge of the fundamental meaning of the sutras and tantras. Saraha admitted him to monastic vows at the Buddhist university of Nalanda. Author of innumerable treatises on the ultimate thought of the Buddha, notably on the authentic meaning of transcendent knowledge and the Middle Way, Nagarjuna did not neglect the medical, alchemical, and political sciences. Among his numerous disciples are Aryadeva and Buddhapalita. Builder of temples and stupas, Nagarjuna was seemingly unlimited in his activities. Tradition has it that he lived six hundred years (thus, to the fifth century of our era). The Nyingmapa school of Tibetan Buddhism holds that he lived to the tenth century.

Naropa: Great scholar and accomplished yogi (1016–1100), disciple of Tilopa and master of Marpa the Translator. His "six yogas" address the bardo, the clear light, the illusory body, the dream, the transfer of consciousness, and inner warmth.

Nirvana (Tib., *myang-'das*): The beyond suffering.

Nonvirtuous acts, ten (Tib., *mi-dge-ba bcu*): The harmful acts. Divided into three acts concerning the body—murder, theft, and sexual misconduct; four acts involving the word—lying, calumny, violent words, and gossip; and three acts related to the mind—covetousness, ill will, and mistaken views.

Omniscience (*sarvajnata; kun-mkhyen*): Synonym for perfect Awakening. Omniscience is not an encyclopedic knowledge or a supermemory but the realization of the emptiness of everything and the knowledge of the attributes, or particularities, of each thing.

Prasanga (Tib., *thal 'gyur*): Literally, "there will/would be error." A form of reasoning consisting in taking up the extremist theses and developing them in all logic to their consequences, which are always seen to be absurd.

Prasangika (Tib., *thal-'gyur-pa*): The adepts of Prasanga, who constitute the loftiest, as well as the most radical, school of Madhyamika, or Middle Way.

Samkhya: A school of Hindu philosophy (sixth century B.C.E.) that underlies the Yoga system and posits two basic metaphysical principles, soul and matter (or nature).

Samsara (Tib., *'khor-ba*): The vicious cycle of deaths and rebirths.

Sautrantika (Tib., *mDo-sde-pa*): Philosophical school of the Lesser Vehicle which, referring to the sutras (and not to their commentaries), accepts the real existence of consciousness and its objects.

Shakyamuni (Tib., *Shakya thub-pa*): "Ascetic of the clan of the Shakyas," the so-called historical Buddha, who lived around the sixth century B.C.E.

Shantideva (Tib., *zhi ba lha*): Great Indian poet and accomplished yogi of the seventh century at the monastic university of Nalanda. His poem *Bodhicharyavatara* (*Way of the Bodhisattva*) exemplifies the teachings of the Madhyamika school.

Spirit of Awakening (*bodhicitta; byang-chub-kyi sems*): The spiritual force accompanying the vow to attain to the Great Awakening for the good of all animate beings, as well as the actual practice of the transcendent virtues leading to omniscience.

Sutra (Tib., *mdo*): Literally, "aphorisms," a general term denoting the discourses of the Buddha Shakyamuni.

Svatantrika (Tib., *rang-rgyud-pa*): A school of Madhyamikas who accept objective existence on the level of conventional truth.

Tantra (*guhyamantra; gsang-sngags, rgud*): Secret formulas, the basic text of the Diamond Vehicle, or Tantric Buddhism; subgroup of the vehicle whose practices are founded on the primordial purity of our veritable nature; practice of the extraordinary union of methods and knowledge. The practices of the tantras are divided into four stages: (1) *kriya* in which the emphasis falls on ritual activities; (2) *carya*, in which these activities are combined with the natural state of deity; (3) *yoga,* in which this natural state is shared with the deity; and (4) *anuttara* ("unsurpassable"), in which the natural state of the deity and that of the adept have never been distinct things. The *anuttara* is divided into father, mother, and neither father nor mother: in other words, into *maha*, in which the accent is on the phase of creation; *anu,* in which it falls on the phase of perfection; and *ati*, or Great Perfection (Tib., *rdzogs-pa chen-po*).

Transcendences (*paramita; pha-rol-tu phyin-pa*): The six transcendent virtues—generosity, discipline, patience, courage, concentration, and knowledge. These virtues are transcendent to the extent that the bodhisattva practices them in the light of direct knowledge of emptiness.

Vaibhashika (Tib., *bye-brag-tu smra-ba*): Philosophical school of the Lesser Vehicle accepting the real existence of objects present, past, and future.

Vasubandhu (Tib., *dbYig-gnyen*): One of the Six Ornaments of the World, brother of Asanga and author of the *Treasury of Scholasticism*. First a disciple of the Cachemirian master

Sanghabhadra, he abandoned the thought of the Lesser Vehicle to place himself in his brother's school, with a special emphasis on Chittamatra. Among his disciples are the logician Dingnaga and the scholastic Sthiramati.

Vehicle (*yana; theg-pa*): Teachings enabling one to traverse the way, that is, to practice.

Veils, two: The veil of the negative emotions (or "emotional veil," *kleshavarana; nyon-sgrib*) and the veil of ignorance (or "cognitive veil," *jneyavarana; shes-sgrib*), both of which obscure primordial wisdom.

Ways, five gradual (*pancamarga; lam-lnga*): The five "stems" of the way leading to the authentic and perfect Awakening.